GW00579287

THE ROYAL NAVY AT MALTA

VOLUME TWO:
1907 - 1939

*A collection of old photographs
taken by the Ellis family
at Malta*

Compiled by
LT CDR BEN WARLOW RN

MARITIME BOOKS

First published in 1990 by
Maritime Books, Lodge Hill,
Liskeard, Cornwall, U.K.

ISBN 0 907771 48 3

Typeset and printed in Great Britain by
Penwell Limited, Callington, Cornwall.

PREFACE

THIS second volume of photographs is a selection from those taken by the Ellis family of Malta during the period from the turn of the century until the outbreak of the Second World War. The photographs have been printed from glass negatives which miraculously survived the heavy bombing suffered by Malta during that war, and, as with the first volume, there can be seen some slight damage. However the overall quality and interest of the scenes is such that even despite the blemishes the damaged photographs have been considered worthy of inclusion. During this period the Royal Navy was consolidating the Nineteenth Century innovations of fast destroyers, and developing the new submarines and aircraft. The learning process was accelerated by the First World War, which, although still fought with battlefleets, nevertheless saw the coming into prominence of submarine warfare and the usefulness of air power, especially in the maritime role. Malta played a significant part in the First World War, the waters nearby being the setting for the first naval incident of that war, the chase of the *Goeben* and *Breslau* in August, 1914. Later its harbours saw the ships heading for the Middle East, and, in particular, for the Gallipoli campaign. Even after the withdrawal from the Dardanelles the pace of the war in the Mediterranean continued with action in the Middle East and the Adriatic, 25 enemy submarines being sunk there in the last 18 months of the war. Once the war was over, operations in the Aegean and the Black Sea kept the Fleet at Malta busy. Throughout these years Malta was the haven for rest and repairs between actions, operations or exercises and, some might add, between fleet cruises. It is hard to imagine that this peace was so savagely shattered in the Second World War, and that Malta ceased to be a haven for embattled ships, but itself became the target for a sustained and vigorous assault, which, by good fortune and by the Herculean efforts of its Maltese and British defenders, it survived. It is hoped that this volume will show the development of the Royal Navy through these busy years.

M.A. CRITCHLEY
Publisher

GRAND HARBOUR
1 December 1908

DRESSED overall in honour of Queen Alexandra's birthday are the *Exmouth* and *Aboukir*. The *Exmouth*, at the head of the line, has few men on her upper deck, whilst the *Aboukir* has her bridge wings lined with Royal Marines. It is interesting to compare the sizes of the *Exmouth*, a *Duncan* Class Battleship completed in May 1903, with the contemporary *Cressy* Class Armoured Cruiser, completed in April 1902. The *Aboukir* was longer and narrower than the battleship, displacing only about one thousand tons less, but with six more boilers and she was two knots faster. The *Duncans* had sacrificed protection for speed, carrying 675 tons of armour less than the previous battleship classes to gain an extra knot. The *Aboukir* carried a single 9.2 inch gun forward and aft whilst the battleship mounted twin 12 inch guns fore and aft. However, both ships carried secondary armaments of twelve 6 inch guns. Another photograph of the *Exmouth* is on page 17, whilst a photograph of the *Aboukir* appears in Volume 1 (page 122). Since the earlier photograph of the *Aboukir* was taken, she had been fitted with fire control tops on her foremasts. There are also differences in the stowages for the stocked anchors, the battleship having a specially cut out bed fitted by the forward turret, whilst the cruiser has hers catted. The introduction of stockless anchors, already in service and fitted in two of the *Duncan* Class, saved considerable work by the cable parties.

H.M.S. TRIUMPH

Above and previous pages

HMS TRIUMPH
2 June 1909 and 1 April 1910

IN the photograph above, taken from the bow, the *Triumph* was seen as she was sailing for Gibraltar in June 1909. She, and her sister ship the *Swiftsure* (see page 15), were an unusual pair of coastal defence ships built for Chile, but purchased by the British Government in 1903. They were very fast as battleships, *Triumph* reaching 20.1 knots over six runs of the measured mile. The view of her on the previous page was taken in April 1910 as she sailed for Suda Bay with the *Russell, Cornwallis* and the *Medea*. Built by Vickers at Barrow, she had slightly lower cowls and heavier funnel caps than her sister, and a smaller medallion in her bow scroll. She was more readily distinguishable, however, by the small protective huts on either bridge wing, seen here with searchlights fitted on top of them. She also carried stockless anchors, although fitted for the stocked type. In 1913 she had gone to Hong Kong to relieve the *Tamar*, and when war broke out she was in reserve there. She was commissioned using the crews of the river gunboats and also two officers, 100 men and six signallers from the Second Battalion Duke of Cornwall's Light Infantry for operations at Tsingtau, where the German forts were captured. In 1915 she was sent to the Dardanelles and was present at the bombardment in February and March. On 25 May submarine U21 fired two torpedoes which passed through her torpedo nets and hit her. She capsized after only 10 minutes and 73 men were lost. 500 men were rescued by the destroyer *Chelmer* (see page 21). The Australian and New Zealand troops offered a month's pay to assist with her salvage in recognition of the good work she had undertaken, but it was not possible to recover her.

HMS BACCHANTE
April 1909

THE *Cressy* Class Armoured Cruiser *Bacchante* was pictured here leaving Grand Harbour for Catania. She accompanied the Royal Yacht the *Victoria and Albert* to Palermo before returning to Malta in May. Her single 9.2 inch gun turret on the forecastle is almost hidden behind the mass of men fallen in in white trousers and blue jumpers, whilst one man is heaving the lead on a platform under the bridge wings. The plates designed to cover the lower end of the hawse pipes to prevent the sea rising up through them can be seen here, ready to be lowered into position. The *Bacchante* had been completed in November 1902 on the Clyde, and then spent the next ten years in the Mediterranean, except for a short period in 1905-6 when she was at Portsmouth with a nucleus crew. At the outbreak of war she was the flagship of the 7th Cruiser Squadron operating in the North Sea. She was absent from the squadron in September when her three sisters, *Hogue*, *Aboukir* and *Cressy* were torpedoed. She was then sent to protect convoys to Gibraltar, and later to the Dardanelles. During the Anzac landings on 25 April 1915, she steamed close inshore until her forefoot was aground, and then provided gunfire support for the troops. In the December she was in reserve in Kaphalo whilst her captain (Captain ADEH Boyle) was in charge of the evacuation of Anzac Cove. She then served on the West African coast before paying off in April 1919, the last of her class in commission. She was sold in 1920.

H.M.S. SUFFOLK

R.ELLIS

HMS SUFFOLK
October 1909

THE *Suffolk* is seen here lying at Malta prior to sailing for Phalerum to relieve her sister ship the *Lancaster*. A *Monmouth* Class Cruiser, of 9800 tons, she had been launched at Portsmouth Dockyard in January 1903. She was the fastest of her class of ten ships on trials, reaching 24.7 knots. She served in the Mediterranean from her completion in 1904 until 1912, and then joined the North American and West Indies Squadron. She was the flagship of Admiral Cradock, being relieved by the *Good Hope*. On 6th August she chased the *Karlsruhe* but was outpaced by the faster German ship. She captured a German merchant ship on 8th August 1914. When she reached Halifax on 12th to fuel, the citizens of Halifax gave her a great welcome and assisted in her coaling. Employed on commerce protection, she was refitted in 1917 and then was sent to the China Station. In August 1918, she carried the British Representative of the Allied Naval Force to Vladivostock. She landed some men and guns, and the only British force to reach Czechoslovakia West of the Urals was on an armoured train which mounted two of *Suffolk*'s 12 pounders, manned by members of her crew. In mid October the train was 4350 miles from the ship, a record for men serving away from their parent ship. She paid off at Devonport in 1919, was sold in 1920 and was broken up in Germany in 1922.

HMS CORNWALLIS

November 1909

THE *Cornwallis* lies in Grand Harbour having just arrived from Gibraltar to relieve the *Canopus*. She was a *Duncan* Class Battleship of 14,000 tons, a class built with slightly less protection than previous battleships in order to achieve better speed. The *Cornwallis* was the fastest of her class on trials at 19.56 knots. She had been completed in February 1904 by the Thames Iron Works at Blackwall and served in the Mediterranean on her first commissioning until 1905, and then again from 1910 to 1912. Although visiting Malta when this photograph was taken, she was part of the Atlantic Fleet. Her square foretop contains the range controls fitted between 1905 and 1907, the other ships of the class, except *Albermarle*, were given oval foretops. Note how tightly stopped the half shackle of cable still attached to the bower anchor is to make it lie horizontally. She rejoined the Mediterranean Fleet in January 1915, and fired the first shot in the preliminary bombardment of the Dardanelles on 18th February 1915, and was the last battleship to leave Suvla Bay during the final evacuation in December 1915. Throughout her spell in Dardanelles she fired 500 rounds of 12 inch and 6000 rounds of 6 inch ammunition. In January 1916 she was at the Suez Canal and a year later, on 9th January 1917, she was sunk by U32 south east of Malta. 15 men were killed in the explosions of the three torpedoes that hit her. The remainder of her crew were taken off before she sank.

KING'S BIRTHDAY
November 1909

THE Fleet is seen above in Grand Harbour, dressed overall for the 68th birthday of King Edward VII, who died six months later. In the foreground is the *Canopus* nameship of a class of 12 inch battleships. She has a two stage accommodation ladder fitted aft to cope with the shelving for the anti-torpedo netting. A month after this picture was taken she left the Mediterranean for the Home Fleet having been relieved by the *Cornwallis*. She returned to the Mediterranean in January 1915 for the Dardanelles operation, just after her action in the Falklands, where she had obtained the first hit on the German Squadron. At the head of the line is the flagship *Exmouth* (see page 17) and astern of her is the cruiser *Lancaster* with the *Duncan* Class Battleship *Russell* at the end of the line. Opposite is another view of the same scene this time with the *Exmouth*, *Lancaster* and *Russell* in line to the left. On the right is the battleship *Triumph* (see page 8) with the *Cressy* Class Cruiser *Aboukir*, completed in April 1902 by Fairfield, ahead of her. *Aboukir* was lost with 527 lives when torpedoed with two of her sister ships by U9 in the North Sea on 22 September 1914.

KING'S BIRTHDAY SEARCHLIGHTS
November 1909

IN this view taken from the inshore end of Grand Harbour and looking seaward, the *Russell* is the ship in the centre, with the remainder of the Fleet ahead of her. The *Triumph* (see page 8) and the cruiser *Aboukir* lie on her port side, and the *Canopus* is to starboard with her masts and funnels showing above the dark, low buildings on the foreshore. The ships used their searchlights for signalling and for night gunnery. They were also used to illuminate attacking torpedo boats and, and hopefully blind them in their glare. In this instance they are being put to a more peaceful use. Later ships were illuminated on special occasions by rows of lamps placed to highlight the ship's silhouette (see page 123). Later still floodlights were introduced, placed away from the ship's side on booms so that the whole of the ship could be seen at night.

HMS MINERVA
10 June 1910

THE *Minerva*, an *Eclipse* Class Cruiser, launched at Chatham Dockyard in September 1895, is seen here entering Grand Harbour on return from exercises with the battlefleet. Originally armed with a mixture of 6 inch and 4.7 inch guns, she was re-equipped prior to this photograph being taken with a uniform armament of eleven 6 inch guns. Economical and successful ships, they were larger that their predecessors in order to improve their seakeeping qualities. Her turtle back forecastle can be seen in this view, part of the weatherly design. After a period in reserve and then with the training squadron, she was attached to the Mediterranean Battle Squadron in 1904 and served there until 1912. At the outbreak of war she was on coastal patrol of the west coast of Ireland and she captured an Austrian merchant ship off Cape Finisterre in September 1914. She was sent to the East Indies in that month, and while there was sent to Akaba to act as an outpost. In March 1915 she arrived at the Dardanelles. On 16th April of that year she forced the Turkish destroyer *Demir Hissar* to beach herself and become a complete wreck. In the August she landed a demonstration force in the Gulf of Xeros before returning to Egyptian waters, later going on to East Africa and the Cape. She was sold in 1920.

HMS SWIFTSURE
10 June 1910

BUILT for coastal defence duties in Chile by Armstrongs at Elswick, and launched on 12 January 1903, she was purchased by the British Government in December 1903. Longer and thinner than contemporary British battleships because of the limited docking facilities available in South America, she had a light main armament of four 10 inch guns, but also carried fourteen 7.5 inch guns. She, and her sister ship the *Triumph*(see page 8), were the only British battleships to carry the 7.5 inch gun. Designed for 19 knots, she achieved 20 knots on six runs of the measured mile, the first British battleship to reach this speed, although there was much vibration at full power. These two ships were easily identified by their narrow funnels and large boat cranes. These cranes gave the ships a great advantage during evolutions. *Swiftsure* had a more prominent ornamental medallion on her bow than *Triumph*. Her bower anchors were of the stocked type, but she carried a stockless sheet anchor on her port side. In November 1914 she was the flagship for the defence of Egypt and later was in action with the Turks at Kantara. Soon afterwards she went to the Dardanelles and was in action again during the attack on the Narrows and supporting the landings. She was placed in reserve in Britain and in 1918 she was converted into a blockship, but was not used as such. Instead she became a target in 1919 before being sold in 1920.

TORPEDO BOAT 64
May 1914

This Yarrow built torpedo boat was built in 1886. She displaced 75 tons and was 125 feet long. Her Commanding Officer was Chief Gunner JW Cottrell, and it must have been an enjoyable command, having a crew of 16 men and a boat capable of 20 knots. On the night 21st March 1915, TB 64 was wrecked on the east side of Lemnos in a North Easterly gale and in low visibility. The Royal Naval Canteen can be seen by Customs House landing in this photograph, with the lift to the Barracca Gardens visible above TB 64's bow.

TORPEDO BOATS
12 October 1911

Five of the early torpedo boats are seen heading out of Malta for exercises in a choppy sea, with a destroyer of the second group of the E (or *River*) Class beyond. The non standard variety of these small vessels made operating together difficult. It also affected their maintenance and support. Armed with several 3 pounder guns and carrying 3 or 5 torpedo tubes, they provided good experience for young officers, giving them the chance to act independently and learn how to handle ships. The later torpedo boats, built about 1906, were about four times the size and comparable with the earlier destroyers, and at that point in their evolution, this type of vessel was discontinued.

HMS EXMOUTH
28 December 1911

Here the *Exmouth*, Flagship of Admiral Sir Edmund Poe KCB KCVO, the Commander-in-Chief, Mediterranean, is seen entering Grand Harbour. A *Duncan* Class Battleship, built by Lairds at Birkenhead and completed in May 1903, her oval foretop with the ranging equipment can be contrasted with her sister ship *Cornwallis* (see page 11). At one time she held the record of 36 seconds for putting out her torpedo nets. In 1904 she was the Flagship of the Home Fleet, and the Admiral, Sir Arthur ('Ard 'Eart') Wilson, went to the foot of her gangway and brought the fleet into Arosa Bay in a fog. In October 1914, she attempted to tow the sinking battleship *Audacious* (see page 44). In November 1914 she took part in the bombardment of Zeebrugge, and was specially fitted with heavy anti-torpedo nets for operations in the Dardanelles in May 1915. She had been sent to the Dardanelles to use the experience she had gained in bombardments off the Belgian Coast. She survived the war and was sold in January 1920, her hull being broken up in Holland in 1922.

Overleaf

HMS CUMBERLAND
February 1912

The *Cumberland* is seen here at Malta when employed as a Cadets' Training Ship. She had arrived from Devonport via Gibraltar and Tangiers on 5th and sailed again on 13th for Port Said and Platea. She had twin, electrically operated 6 inch turrets on the forecastle and quarterdeck, whilst there were five 6 inch mounted singly on each side. The twin turret proved cramped and liable to electrical defects, and its weight forward caused the ships to pitch heavily in a seaway. However, they were generally good seaboats, designed for 23 knots, which many exceeded by almost 2 knots. In an Atlantic race by 6 cruisers in November 1905, *Cumberland* came a close third. The winner was the *Drake*, who averaged 18.504 knots from Sandy Hook to Tarifa Point, and the second ship, the *Berwick*, was only 1600 yards astern at the end of the race. The state of her funnels indicate she has recently had some hard steaming. In 1914 she took part in operations off the Cameroons, capturing 10 enemy ships at Duala. Her field guns were used ashore in the campaign and her marines and boats were employed in the river operations. In December 1914, she left the area, but her Captain remained to conduct operations. She also left behind guns, steamboats and other equipment. She spent a period with the Grand Fleet and then was employed on convoy escort duties. After the war she returned to her training role until 1921, when she paid off and was sold.

HMS YARMOUTH
8 July 1912

THE *Yarmouth* was a *Weymouth* Class Light Cruiser, a follow on from the *Bristol* Class, the main improvement being a uniform armament of eight 6 inch guns, instead of a mixture of 6 inch and 4 inch. Built by London and Glasgow, Govan, she was completed in April 1912 and had just arrived on the station after commissioning at Chatham. Having visited Crete in June, she is seen here sailing from Grand Harbour for Platea, with her crew in whites and wearing sennet hats, the awnings being kept rigged against the hot Mediterranean summer sun. The smoke from the second funnel would be unpopular with the Captain, and more so with the Commander who would be watching his awnings and paintwork. The red bands of her centre funnels identifying her are hardly visible in this picture. Whilst the others of her class had four propellers driven by Parsons turbines, *Yarmouth* had only two, driven by Brown Curtis turbines. Designed for 25 knots, the class all exceeded this by between half and one knot on trials. At the outbreak of war she was at Wei Hei Wei, and took part in the search for the *Emden*. She was at the Battle of Jutland. In June 1917 Flt Cdr F J Rutland successfully flew off a Sopwith Pup from an experimental platform fitted on her weather deck. On 21 August 1917, the *Yarmouth* lured Zeppelin L53 out to sea, then launched her aircraft, which shot it down. As a result of this success 22 light cruisers were fitted with flying off platforms. She was sold in 1929.

HMS CHELMER
3 November 1912

THE *River* (or E) Class Destroyers designers gave priority to seaworthiness, and the 550 ton *Chelmer*, one of the Thornycroft built members of the class, shows her lines here. She was equipped with Thornycroft-Schultz boilers and reached 25.70 knots on trials. Her high forecastle shows the real break between the earlier destroyers and torpedo boats and the new destroyers. Her forward 12 pounder is mounted on a bandstand high above the forecastle and she has a separate bridge. The class were given stronger hulls than previous vessels, and also the officers were given separate cabins. Hip baths were introduced too, and perhaps 'old salts' said that things were becoming soft in destroyers. Here she is seen under the command of Lieutenant and Commander G C Dickens, who later commanded the *Harpy* (see page 39). At the outbreak of war she was at Hong Kong, but returned to the Mediterranean and was involved in the Dardanelles operations in 1915. She landed troops at Anzac Cove and helped to rescue the crew of the *Ocean* when she was sunk. She also rescued over 500 men from the *Triumph* (see page 8) when she was lost. During one rescue operation she was damaged, having 18 feet of her bottom blown in and her centre boiler room flooded. Repairs were completed at the Dardanelles by the staff of the Depot Ship *Blenheim* (see page 84). During the campaign she wore out her 12 pounder, firing 1375 rounds in support of the troops ashore. Her other guns were so worn that they were virtually howitzers. She was detached from the Aegean Squadron in January 1918 and then operated in the Adriatic. She was sold in June 1920.

HMS FOAM
November 1912

THE destroyer *Foam* is seen here lying off Fort St Angelo, flying the flag of Rear Admiral Sackville H. Carden, who was the Admiral Superintendent at Malta at the time. The *Foam* was a tender to the *Egmont*, the Base Ship at Malta, and she had been selected to wear the Admiral's flag. One of ten Thornycroft built 30 knot destroyers which were later categorised in the D Class, she was launched in October 1896. They were built of high tensile steel to save weight. One of the class, the *Angler*, was quoted as running so smoothly at 30 knots that a glass of water filled to 5/8 inch from the top was not spilt. She carried a 12 pounder gun forward, and five 6 pounders along her upper deck, and aft she had two 18 inch torpedo tubes. Another of the class, the *Ariel*, was wrecked on the breakwater at Malta in 1907. The *Foam* was sold in 1914, being broken up in Norway. The remainder of the class served in the war, *Coquette* being mined in the North Sea in March 1916, the others surviving to be sold afterwards. Beyond her bow can be seen the breakwater to Grand Harbour, completed only three years before with the even more recent addition of a lighthouse on its seaward end.

HMS ALBATROSS
November 1912

THE *Albatross* was launched by Thornycroft on 19th July 1898. She displaced 360 tons and was capable of 31.75 knots. When the early destroyers were classified in 1913, she was placed in the C Class (having 3 funnels and being capable of 30 knots). She was one of three vessels ordered in 1896-7 as '33 knot specials'. They were built with longer and more expensive hulls in order to achieve this high speed. *Albatross* came closest and much effort and money was spent from October 1898 to July 1900 trying to make her go faster. The three funnel arrangement was unusual for Thornycroft vessels of this period, and arose out of these trials. The other two vessels were the *Express* (Lairds) which reached 31 knots and the *Arab* (Thomson) which reached 30.75 knots. A collapsible boat lies at her boom, whilst another is on the upper deck by her forefunnel uncovered, and a third is covered beside her second funnel. She returned to home waters in November 1913, when the G Glass Destroyers arrived on station. She survived the war and was sold in June 1920.

HMS AFRICA

November 1912

THE *Africa* is seen here leaving harbour in the same 'cleared for action' state as the *King Edward VII* (see page 27), but without the hammocks placed for protection. She has a screw flagsman visible on a platform above the starboard after 9.2 inch gun turret, and a guard saluting on her quarterdeck. Her 12 pounders amidships have light shields instead of being open. The *Africa* was launched by Chatham Dockyard on 20th May 1905, and was the first battleship fitted with a forced lubrication system in her engines. It was so successful that it was installed in the remainder of her class, and also in older battleships. The class was fitted with a variety of boilers for comparative trials, *Africa* having 12 Babcock and 3 cylindrical boilers and reaching 18.95 knots on trials. In December 1911/January 1912, she was engaged on trials with aircraft, launching a Short S27 'Pusher' aircraft from a ramp fitted on her forecastle whilst at anchor. The flight (by Lt C R Samson) was successful, and the aircraft landed on the sea. During the war she served with the Third Battle Squadron of the Grand Fleet, and in 1916 joined the British Adriatic Squadron. In 1917 she undertook convoy work on the West Coast of Africa. She became an accommodation ship in 1919, and was sold in June, 1920.

FLEET LEAVING HARBOUR
9 November 1912

THE *Hibernia*, Flagship of Rear Admiral Cecil F Thursby CMG, leads the *Britannia, Dominion* and *Commonwealth* out of Grand Harbour. They formed half of the Third Battle Squadron of the First Fleet, and were heading to Smyrna whilst the other four battleships of the *King Edward VII* Class which formed the remainder of the Third Battle Squadron sailed separately to operate under the Flagship *King Edward VII*. Each group was escorted by a cruiser, this group by the *Dartmouth*, and the other group by the *Weymouth*. The torpedo net booms sloping upward and aft give the ships the illusion of being fitted with bulges, which they were not. The *Commonwealth* was fitted with bulges in 1918 when employed on bombarding duties. She also had a tripod mast fitted and her six inch guns were removed. The *Britannia* was torpedoed off Cape Trafalgar on 9th November 1918, and remained afloat for $3^{1}/_{2}$ hours before sinking. She and the *King Edward VII* (see page 27) were the only two war losses of this class.

HM QUEEN'S BIRTHDAY
1 December 1912

FIVE of the *King Edward VII* Class Battleships can be seen here in Grand Harbour, dressed overall in honour of the Queen's birthday. The *Hindustan* is in the left foreground, with the *King Edward VII* - then the Flagship (see page 27) on the right foreground. *Hibernia*, also Devonport built, is astern of her and *Africa* (see page 24) is beyond. The eight ships of the class formed the Third Battle Squadron, and four had arrived ten days before from Smyrna to join their sisters. Individual ship differences can be noted, square control tops in *Hibernia*, and oval in *King Edward VII* and *Hindustan*, whilst *Hindustan* has 12 pounders fitted on her forward 12 inch turret. All the class had stockless anchors, and the 9.2 inch guns in single turrets at the fore and after ends of the side batteries were very distinctive.

HMS KING EDWARD VII
December 1912

THE *King Edward VII*, nameship of her class, is seen here leaving Grand Harbour cleared for action, with hammocks placed around the upper bridge and exposed guns amidships to protect the men at these quarters. Fitted with three main sizes of gun, 12 inch, 9.2 inch and 6 inch, the class were at a disadvantage for monitoring their fire, and in the following class (the *Lord Nelsons*) the six inch guns were omitted. They were the first battleships fitted with balanced rudders since 1870, and they could turn in a 340 yard circle at 15 knots. They were, however, difficult to keep on a steady course and became known as 'The Wobbley Eight'. Fighting tops were omitted in the design, and gun control platforms fitted instead. The after bridge was also discontinued with this class. *King Edward VII* was launched at Devonport by the King in July 1903 who directed that she should always be a Flagship. Here she is seen as the Flagship of Vice Admiral Cecil Burney, being in the Third Battle Squadron of the First Fleet. She was mined on 6th January 1916, when on her way from Scapa to Belfast for a refit, and for the first time a private ship and not a Flagship. She hit a mine laid by the *Moewe* and both her engine rooms flooded. There was a strong wind and the sea was rising. She was first taken in tow by the collier *Melita,* then by the leader *Kempenfelt*, but it was finally realised that she could not be saved and her crew were taken off by four destroyers, no one being lost. It took 13 hours before she sank, a tribute to her good stability.

HMS BLACK PRINCE
27 February 1913

IN this stern view of the *Black Prince*, lying in Bighi Bay, she is seen getting under way to head for the Syrian coast to relieve her sister ship the *Duke of Edinburgh*. She herself had recently arrived on the Station from Portsmouth. She was one of the first cruisers fitted to spray oil fuel onto the coal fired furnaces to improve consumption. Although this increased the smoke given off, she was a fast steamer, achieving 23.65 knots on trials on the Polperro measured mile in good weather. She had six single 9.2 inch guns, the starboard side after gun can be seen in this view, mounted on the upper deck above a 6 inch gun. The 6 inch secondary armament was mounted very low and was badly affected by any sea. In March 1916, these low 6 inch gun ports were closed and six 6 inch guns with shields were mounted on the upper deck instead. At the outbreak of war she was in the Mediterranean and was involved in the chase of the *Goeben* and *Breslau*. Soon afterwards she was sent to the Red Sea where she captured two Hamburg Amerika ships, the *Istria* and *Sudmark*. In the November she was ordered home to the Grand Fleet to replace the battlecruisers being sent to the South Atlantic. She remained with the Grand Fleet and was damaged early in the action at Jutland and was finally overwhelmed and blew up on 1st June, 857 officers and men being lost in her.

HMS PROSERPINE
March 1913

THE *Proserpine* is seen here sailing for Alexandretta. She was a third class cruiser of 2135 tons, a member of the *Pelorus* Class of 11 ships, which were chosen for comparative trials of the various boilers available at that time. Designed for 20 knots, their speed soon deteriorated as most had boiler trouble, and several only served for a few years. They had a raised forecastle and poop deck, which led to their being wet amidships, and their narrow beam caused them to roll heavily. Their armament was eight four inch guns, two side by side on the forecastle and poop and the others in the waist. The lighter 4 inch was chosen instead of the 4.7 inch gun in the previous (*Pearl*) Class to compensate for the narrower beam, which was designed to improve their speed. She had been launched at Sheerness Dockyard in December 1896, and from completion in 1899 had served on the North American and West Indies Station and later in the East Indies. She arrived on the Mediterranean Station in 1913, and soon afterwards returned to Sheerness. When war broke out she took the Plymouth Battalion to Ostend and then patrolled off Gibraltar. When the heavy, armoured cruisers were recalled to the Grand Fleet to replace the battlecruisers sent to the Falklands, *Proserpine* was one of the smaller cruisers sent out to replace them in Egyptian waters. She patrolled off the Syrian coast and was the only British ship left at the Canal after most of the Fleet had been sent to the Dardanelles in April 1915. She remained in that area, and was sold at Alexandria in 1919, being broken up at Genoa in 1923.

HMS DEFENCE
28 May 1913

IN this view the *Defence* is sailing from Grand Harbour flying the flag of Rear Admiral E C T Troubridge CB CMG MVO, Rear Admiral Commanding the First Cruiser Squadron. She has a twin 9.2 inch turret forward and aft, whilst along her sides are her secondary armament of ten 7.5 inch guns in single turrets. Built at Pembroke Dock, and completed in February 1909, she was one of the three *Minotaur* Class armoured cruisers of 14600 tons, designed for 23 knots. Originally built with low funnels, the funnels were raised by 15 feet by the time this photograph was taken. She had just returned from the China Station where she and her sister the *Minotaur* had met the *Scharnhorst* and *Gneisenau*, and in friendly rivalry agreed that if they met in action the British ships would not use one 7.5 inch gun to make it a fair fight. She was involved in the search for the *Goeben* and *Breslau* in the Mediterranean at the outbreak of the war. Later she was ordered to join Admiral Cradock's squadron in the South Atlantic but was diverted to the Dardanelles, finally heading South too late to join Admiral Cradock. She transferred her Poulsen wireless equipment to the *Invincible* for the Falklands action - whilst the *Vindictive*, which had similar equipment - was ordered to Ascension Island to keep the battle-cruiser squadron in direct contact with England. She joined the Grand Fleet in 1915, and was Admiral Arbuthnot's flagship at Jutland, where she was lost with all 893 men. It was believed by some that these ships sacrificed armour for weight of armament, and three of the type were lost from Admiral Arbuthnot's squadron, at Jutland, only the *Duke of Edinburgh* (see page 33) surviving.

H.M.S. DEFENCE

H·M·S·BELLEROPHON

HMS BELLEROPHON
November 1913

NAMESHIP of her class of battleships, the *Bellerophon* is seen here leaving Malta for Alexandria, and then for passage to Salamis Bay. As the next class to be built after the *Dreadnought*, the *Bellerophons* had a completely different mast arrangement, and also carried a more powerful secondary armament of sixteen 4 inch guns. This was the first class fitted with anti-torpedo bulkheads, and their high masts were for wireless aerials. Later the height of the masts was reduced as wireless technology improved. She is seen here with an experimental searchlight grouping around her fore and main masts. A good steamer, she achieved 21.8 knots on trials and over 22 knots later. In this view screens can be seen fitted around the 4 inch guns mounted on the wing 12 inch gun turrets. Later all the secondary armament was mounted in the superstructure and an anti-aircraft gun was fitted aft. Flying off platforms for aircraft were added to A and Y turrets in 1917. At the time this photograph was taken she was part of the First Battle Squadron under Captain E F Bruen, having commissioned at Devonport in April 1913. At the outbreak of war she was en route to Gibraltar for a refit. She served in the Grand Fleet throughout the war and was present at Jutland as part of the Fourth Battle Squadron, still under Captain Bruen. In 1919 she was placed in reserve and became a turret drill ship at Sheerness before being sold in 1921. She was broken up in Germany in September 1922.

HMS DUKE OF EDINBURGH
November 1913

THE *Duke of Edinburgh* was the nameship of the first of three classes of armoured cruiser, in which a heavy gun armament and high speed were given priority. She is seen here leaving Grand Harbour for Palermo and to carry out evolutions on passage. The size of her ship's company was 798 men, many of whom can be seen amidships. The accommodation was very cramped and uncomfortable because of the large numbers onboard. A Royal marine guard can be seen paraded on her quarterdeck. She was launched at Pembroke Dock in 1904, and on completion served in home waters. In 1913 she joined the Mediterranean Fleet and was there at the outbreak of war when her squadron was involved in the chase of the *Goeben* and *Breslau*. Shortly afterwards she was sent to the Red Sea, where she captured the German *Altair*. In November 1914, she led the force that captured Fort Tumba, bombarding the fort and covering the landings at Sheikh Syed. She then joined the Grand Fleet and was present at Jutland, being the only survivor of her squadron. By then her low 6 inch battery had been removed, and six 6 inch guns were mounted in shields on the upper deck, where they could be worked when the weather was rough. Two more 6 inch guns were mounted on the forecastle later, and the foremast was converted to a tripod. She served on convoy duties in 1917 and 1918, and was paid off in 1919, being broken up at Blyth in 1920.

HMS INFLEXIBLE

THE *Inflexible* was the second battlecruiser of the *Invincible* Class, being built at Clydebank, completing in October 1908. Designed for the then high speed of 25 knots, she achieved 25.5 knots on trials and later all the class were credited with reaching 28 knots once they had shaken down. Much of the credit for her speed must go to the stokers who had to feed the boilers with coal, and a group of these men, well scrubbed and in their best suits and sennet hats can be seen in front of her honours board. It is interesting to note that even these hats were worn 'flat aback' by some. The harbour scene (taken in June 1913) shows the ship's mascot on deck alongside the forward twin 12 inch gun turret, with the starboard twin turret visible under the awning. The protective shielding for the 4 inch guns on the turrets can be seen on her A and Y turrets in the picture taken as she leaves harbour. In this view her high freeboard, the highest of any British warship at that time, can be seen, together with the tall forefunnel, which had been extended two years earlier to keep smoke clear of the bridge and fire control positions. At the outbreak of war she was in the Mediterreanean and was involved in the chase of the *Goeben* and *Breslau*. During the Falklands action she fired 560 rounds of ammunition and was hit twice with little damage. On 18 March 1915 at the Dardanelles she was hit repeatedly by shore batteries during the attack on the Narrows, then she struck a mine. She took in 2000 tons of water and lost 32 men, but managed to struggle to Tenedos and then on to Gibraltar for repairs. She was present at Jutland where she "led on boldly" after her sister ship, the *Invincible*, had been lost. She was sold in 1922.

HM SUBMARINE B10
November 1913

THE B Class was the third class of British submarines, and the first fitted with forward hydroplanes. B10 was built by Vickers, as were all the earlier British submarines, being launched in March 1906. The surface propulsion was by means of a petrol engine. Diesel engines were introduced with the D Class (1908-1911) after having been tried in the A13 in 1905. Five of B10's crew of 13 can be seen on the conning tower as she heads out of Grand Harbour. Much of her length is submerged, very much in the style of today's nuclear submarines. The small triangular flag on her stern would appear to be a safety marker so that craft kept well clear of that submerged part, which comprised her rudder and propeller. She and her sisters B9 and B11 took part in the Dardanelles campaign operating from Mudros from August 1914. B11 sank the Turkish cruiser *Messudieh* there on 13th December 1914. B10 was lost on 9 August 1916 when she was bombed at Venice whilst undergoing repairs. Five of the class were converted to surface patrol boats in 1917, with their hulls raised and conning towers replaced by wheelhouses.

HMS INVINCIBLE

18 November 1913

SEEN here sailing from Malta for Alexandria with the *Indomitable* and *Inflexible*, this was *Invincible*'s last voyage with the Mediterranean Fleet, as in December she returned to Portsmouth to pay off. Her guard and band are fallen in by the leadsman under the bridge and not in the usual position on the quarterdeck. Her forefunnel was not raised until February 1915, after the Battle of the Falkland Islands, where she had received 22 hits but had only one casualty. She was the first of the battlecruisers, being built by Armstrongs at Elswick, but her completion was delayed until 1909 by problems with her turrets, which were electrically operated. Hydraulic equipment, which proved to be smoother and more reliable, was installed instead in 1914. She took part in the action off Heligoland on 28th August 1914 in which two German ships were lost, and which had a profound effect on the morale of the German Navy for the rest of the war. During the Falklands action she had one leg of a tripod mast shot away, but the other two legs were strong enough to support the mast. She rejoined the Grand Fleet and was present at the Battle of Jutland. She was Admiral Hood's Flagship in that action, and was engaged by the *Lutzow, Derfflinger* and *Konig*. She was hit in Q turret and the magazine blew up, splitting the ship in two. There were only six survivors, rescued by the destroyer *Badger*. Most of the survivors had been in the control top. The remaining 1026 officers and men were lost.

THE FLEET IN HARBOUR
November 1913

IN the foreground of this picture of the Fleet lying in Grand Harbour is the *Inflexible* (see page 35), wearing the flag of the Commander-in-Chief Mediterranean (Admiral Sir Archibald Berkeley Milne Bt GCVO KCB), and astern of her is the *Indomitable*, then temporarily with the Second Battle Squadron in the Mediterranean. Just after commissioning the *Indomitable* had taken the Prince of Wales to Quebec, and on the return journey had average 25.13 knots from Belle Isle to Fastnet. After the Dogger Bank action in January 1915 she towed the damaged battlecruiser *Lion* home to Rosyth. Astern of her is the *Duncan* Class battelship *Cornwallis* (see page 11) and beyond her is the *Chatham* Class Cruiser *Chathan*.

   The far line of ships is led by the Cruiser *Defence*, of the *Minotaur* Class. She was the Flagship of the First Cruiser Squadron in the Mediterranean, commanded by Rear Admiral E C T Trowbridge CB CMG MVO. Astern of her is the *Dreadnought*, then Flagship of Vice Admiral Sir Charles J Briggs KCB, commanding the Fourth Battle Squadron. During her early trials the *Dreadnought* averaged 21.6 knots on four measured mile runs and had steamed 7000 miles. On the 3400 mile run from Gibraltar to Trinidad she had averaged 17 knots. Another *Chatham* Class Cruiser, the *Dublin*, lies astern of her. Shortly after this photograph was taken the ships sailed in two groups, one for Alexandria and the other for Port Said, and then all met up again in Salamis Bay. There were seven battleships, three battlecruisers, four armoured cruisers, thirteen cruisers and fourteen destroyers in Malta at that time.

HMS HARPY
December 1913

THE *Harpy* is a brave sight as she enters harbour, having just arrived from Devonport in company with the *Wolverine, Beagle, Foxhound* and *Bulldog*, who were to relieve the *Blonde, Garry, Desperate, Stag, Albatross, Foam* and the *Angler. Harpy* was built by Whites, being launched in November 1909 and she was in the first group of the *Basilisk* Class, having a narrower third funnel, unlike the second group (see *Grasshopper* on page 40). She was commanded by Lieutenant and Commander G C Dickens a grandson of the novelist who had previously commanded the *Chelmer* (see page 21). In November 1910 she had stripped her port turbine in heavy weather. She was engaged in the Dardanelles campaign in 1915, patrolling the Cape Helles area. On 25 May 1915 she chased a submarine that was making for a French battleship. The French ship was not attacked, but later the *Vengeance* and the *Swiftsure* were fired at, but not hit. The *Triumph* was also attacked and was sunk. The *Harpy*, like the *Grasshopper*, was sold to Fryer in November 1921.

HMS GRASSHOPPER
January 1914

This view of the *Grasshopper*, a *Basilisk* Class destroyer, shows clearly her upper deck layout, with close stowing anchors set in a high forecastle and the forward 4 inch gun mounted on a deckhouse. The two single torpedo tubes are mounted well aft of the three raked funnels. Built by Fairfield in 1909, she was commanded by Lieutenant and Commander R T Anderson, who was still commanding her in the Dardanelles campaign in 1915. She remained in the Mediterranean throughout. In March 1915 she was one of the destroyers defending the trawler minesweepers, and saw the French battleship *Bouvet* sunk. In April she supported the landings at Morto Bay and in May she saw the battleships *Triumph* and *Majestic* sunk. In May she escorted the submarine E11 (Lt Cdr M Dunbar-Nasmith) on the first leg of her passage to the Sea of Marmara. In the next few months she landed troops at Helles (W) Beach and Suvla. During the evacuation of the Helles area she, with the *Bulldog*, got alongside the hulks at night and by fine seamanship helped rescue 1600 troops. She stayed in the area in 1916 and also in 1917, when she was involved in convoy escort duties. She survived the war and was sold to Fryer, Sunderland, in November 1921.

HMS SAVAGE
February 1914

The *Savage* was a *Basilisk* Class Destroyer built by Thornycroft, being launched on 10 March 1910. She is seen here on her return to Malta after visiting Astakos, Corfu and Dragamesti Bay with her sister ships *Scourge* and *Rattlesnake*. The single 4 inch gun and three 12 pounders she carried gave a $62^{1}/2$ pound broadside. The previous class, the *Tribals*, had had a $37^{1}/2$ to 50 pound broadside. The *Basilisks* carried the larger 21 inch torpedo tubes instead of the earlier 18 inch tubes. A member of the Fifth Flotilla, the *Savage* is carrying the distinguishing funnel bands which were abandoned in favour of pendant numbers, although, later, funnel bands were again brought into use, but the second time to distinguish different flotillas. She has searchlights fitted on the bridge and right aft. She spent part of the war with the Aegean Squadron, being detached for repairs at a home port in January 1918. She was sold to Ward, Portishead, in May 1921.

Overleaf

HM SHIPS RACOON AND BASILISK
January 1914

The two *Basilisk* Class Destroyers are seen moored off Bighi Hospital. The *Basilisk* is on the left, her narrower after funnel indicating she is in the first group of the class, whilst the *Racoon*, with three even funnels is on the right. The *Racoon* has a second searchlight abaft her funnels and does not carry one on her bridge. She had been built by Cammell Laird in 1910, and was engaged in the Dardanelles campaign, being at the first landings in February 1915. Just before that action she had returned to Malta with Admiral Carden after he had been relieved by Admiral de Robeck. In March 1915 she was engaged in defending the minesweepers and in the August was at the landings at Suvla. On 2 September she was the first vessel on the scene when the troopship *Southland* was torpedoed 20 miles south of Mudros. The troopship, of 12,000 tons, was carrying 1400 men and *Racoon* brought her safely to harbour. She was lost with all hands on 9th January 1918 when she ran aground off the West Coast of Ireland in a snowstorm. The *Basilisk* was built by Whites in 1910 and was also employed in the Dardanelles campaign on similar duties to the *Racoon*. In December 1915 she had the task of shelling the abandoned camps at Suvla. In January 1918 she was detached from the Aegean Squadron and in May 1918 she, with the USS *Lydonia*, sank U70 south of the Balearic Islands. She was sold in November 1921.

R.ELLIS

H.M.S.BASILISK

H·M·S·RACOON

R.ELLIS

H.M.S. AUDACIOUS

HMS AUDACIOUS
February 1914

BUILT at Lairds, and completed four months before this photograph was taken, the *Audacious* was one of the *King George V* Class Battleships. She, with her sister *Ajax* (see page 46) was completed with the director tower at the mast head, entailing the strengthening of the foremast with tripods reaching half way up the mast. The *Centurion* was modified to this rig, but the *King George V* was fitted with strengthening flanges instead. The *Audacious* had a very short career, for on 27 October 1914, a year after completion, she hit a mine laid by the *Berlin*, a converted merchant liner of 12000 tons, off Tory Island. Her port engine room was quickly flooded and the centre engine room was also partly flooded. The cruiser *Liverpool* stood by her, assisted by the tugs which had been towing targets for the squadron's gunnery practice. She managed to get under way, but was down by the stern. Efforts were made to tow her by the liner *Olympic,* the collier *Thornhill* and the battleship *Exmouth* (see page 17), but as she settled towing became impossible. Her crew were taken off by the *Olympic. Audacious* suddenly blew up, and the only casualty of the whole operation was sustained then, a Petty Officer in the *Liverpool* being killed by falling debris. Her sinking was kept secret because of the current Turkish crisis.

R.ELLIS   H·M·S·BOADICEA

HMS BOADICEA
February 1914

THE Scout Cruiser *Boadicea* was attached to the Second Battle Squadron, and is seen here following the *Ajax* (see page 46) out of Grand Harbour and enroute to Corfu. Of 3500 tons, she was launched at Pembroke Dock in May 1908 and achieved 25.75 knots on trials. Hers was the first class of cruisers fitted with turbine engines. Lightly armed with only six 4 inch guns, one pair were on the forecastle, another pair on the upper deck by the break of the forecastle and a third pair aft. The port midships and after guns are visible in this photograph. A further four 4 inch guns were fitted amidships in 1916, and a 3 inch anti-aircraft gun was mounted on the quarterdeck. She had two torpedo tubes, the port one of which can be seen mounted on the deck between the forward cutter and whaler. In November 1917 she was converted to carry 66 mines and was attached to the Battle Squadron of the Grand Fleet. Placed in reserve in 1919 at the Nore, she was put into harbour service at Dartmouth in 1921 to replace the *Pomone* (1897), which had been there since 1910. She was to have taken *Pomone*'s name, but retained her own. She was sold in July 1926 for breaking up at Rosyth.

HMS AJAX
February 1914

THE *Ajax* is seen here leaving Grand Harbour for Corfu following her sisters the *Audacious* (see page 44) and the *King George V* (nameship of the class) (see page 85). With the *Orion* Class Battleship *Conqueror*, seen ahead of the *Ajax*, they formed the Second Battle Squadron and had sailed from Malta from Portland, visiting Vigo, Arosa Bay and Gibraltar on the way out. Built by Scotts and completed in March 1913, *Ajax* displaced 23,000 tons and carried ten 13.5 inch guns, with a secondary armament of sixteen 4 inch guns. All the class were good steamers, capable of 22 knots, whilst *Ajax* achieved 22.47 knots on trials. The lack of a heavier secondary armament brought much criticism. In the *Dreadnought* the Officers' quarters had been moved forward. With this class the officers once more returned aft, as can be seen from the sternwalk. *Ajax* served with the Grand Fleet during the war and was present at Jutland. In 1919 she joined the Mediterranean Fleet. She, with the *Centurion* was under Admiral Sir John de Robeck in the Black Sea when General Denikers' operations against the Bolsheviks failed. The fleet was employed evacuating important people. In 1924 she was placed in reserve and was taken to Rosyth in December 1926 to start her breaking up which was completed at Charlestown.

HMS INDEFATIGABLE
2 March 1914

THE second class of battlecruisers were longer than the first in order to improve the arcs of fire of the main armament of 12 inch guns. The overall appearance was also improved by leading the tripods aft on both masts and by the removal of the clutter of the boat stowage that was around the after mast of the *Invincible*s (see page 37). The *Indefatigable* was built at Devonport Dockyard, where the slip had to be lengthened by 90 feet to cope with her length. She is seen in this view lying in Grand Harbour, with a church service in progress. Soon afterwards she sailed for Genoa, then went on to Elba and Naples. She was still in the Mediterranean in August, during the chase of the *Goeben* and *Breslau*. She took part in the Dardanelles blockade, but was relieved in January, 1915, when she returned to home waters and joined the Grand Fleet. At Jutland she engaged in a duel with the *Vonn der Tann*. She was hit and was staggering out of the line when she was hit again and she exploded. 1017 officers and men were lost. There were two survivors who were rescued by a German destroyer and became prisoners of war.

HMS EGMONT
May 1914

ORIGINALLY an Iron Screw Ship, built at Chatham Dockyard and launched as the *Achilles* in 1863, she had ceased her seagoing career in 1885, having been regarded as one of the best fighting ships in her time. She lay dismantled in the Hamoaze until 1902, when she was towed to Malta to become the Depot Ship there, replacing the old wooden wall *Hibernia*, whose name she took. She was renamed *Egmont* in March, 1904 and continued to serve as the Depot Ship in Malta until 1914. She paid off on 4th May, and the new base was commissioned on the 5th, the gunboat *Firefly* being renamed to carry the base ship name. On 16th May, the old *Egmont* was brought out of harbour by the paddle tug *Cracker. (The Cracker* had been built in 1900 by the London and Glasgow Eng & Iron SB Co and was based on Malta from 1911. Her coal fired engines drove her two independent paddle wheels which were fitted with feathering blades. She was at Sheerness for a period before being broken up in 1956). Once clear of the harbour, the *Egmont* was taken in tow by the cruiser *Black Prince* (see page 28), who took her to Gibraltar. From Gibraltar the battleship *Britannia* took over the tow, taking her to Sheerness. The *Egmont* was recommissioned as the *Egremont* in June 1916 and was used as the base at Chatham. She was renamed *Pembroke* in June 1919. She was sold in January 1923, 60 years after being launched.

GRAND HARBOUR
May 1914

THE three British battlecruisers in line on the right of this scene are saluting for Queen Mary's birthday. The *Inflexible* (see page 35) is the Commander-in-Chief's Flagship at the head of the line, whilst astern of her are the *Indomitable*, a sister ship of the *Inflexible,* and the *Indefatigable* (see page 47), of the second class of battlecruisers. *Indomitable* took part in the chase of the *Goeben* and *Breslau* and then the blockade of the Dardanelles prior to returning to Home Waters. After the action at Dogger Bank she took part in the Battle of Jutland. She was sold in 1922. The bow of the Admiral's yacht, the ex Torpedo gunboat *Hussar* (see Volume I, page 93 and page 70) can be seen beyond the fortifications of Senglea. Beyond her, moored under Corradino Heights, is an Austro-Hungarian Squadron on a training cruise. The two leading ships are the newly completed *Viribus Unitis* Class *Dreadnoughts Veribis Unitis* and *Tegettof*. Of 20,000 tons displacement and carrying their twelve 12 inch guns in triple turrets, they reached 21.8 knots on trials. The *Viribus Unitis* was sunk on the night 31 October/1 November 1918 by a fixed torpedo from the Italian *CMB Locusta*. The *Tegettof* was attacked by a French Submarine and later by Italian MAS boats but was unscathed. She was ceded to Italy in 1919 and scrapped at La Spezia in 1924/5. The third Austro-Hungarian ship is the Battleship *Zrinyi* of the *Radetzky* Class. With four 12 inch guns and eight 9.4 inch guns this class was designed for 20 knots but reached 20.58 on trials. She was interned under US Navy control at Spalato in 1919 and was scrapped in Italy in 1920/21.

HMS GLOUCESTER - STOKERS

THIS group of stokers from the cruiser *Gloucester* are seen posing beside the quarterdeck 6 inch gun. They are in their clean tropical rig and hardly hidden from the bright summer sun by the awning. Perhaps this picture was taken after Sunday divisions, and a messdeck bench has been brought up for them to sit on. There seems no standard way for their lanyards to be worn, indeed, the man in the front row on the left does not appear to have a lanyard at all. The sennet hats placed in front of the front row were known as 'Benjies'. The *Gloucester* was a *Bristol* Class Cruiser, completed by Beardmore in October 1910. In August 1914 she was commanded by Captain W A Howard Kelly MVO when she became involved in the chase of the *Goeben* and *Breslau*. Before the war the crews of the *Goeben* and *Gloucester* had been on good terms, playing water polo against each other at Durazzo. The *Gloucester* sighted the German ships on 6th August and shadowed them, engaging both ships on 7th August to keep them together, but finally having to withdraw when very low on fuel. She was the one ship to come through the incident with credit, some of which must be given to the stokers who kept her steaming well throughout the critical period.

HMS SENTINEL ENTERTAINERS 1916

ALTHOUGH both peace and war in the Service had moments of action and excitement, much time had to be passed in humdrum employment in areas where there was little for the men to do but fall back upon their own resources for entertainment. The Scout Cruiser *Sentinel* of 2880 tons and with 268 men was clearly no exception with a large band of musicians and actors. The RNR Lieutenant, with his doubly wavy stripes is in charge, and there is a cross section of gunners, stokers and marines, as well as female impersonators and clowns. The *Sentinel* had arrived in the Mediterranean in 1915 from duty in the North Sea, having started the war with the 6th Destroyer Flotilla at Dover, then transferring to the 8th Destroyer Flotilla operating from the Forth, and later joining the 6th Light Cruiser Squadron on the Humber. She spent the rest of the war in the Mediterranean, the latter part in the Aegean. She paid off at Sheerness in 1919, and was a Mechanics' Training Ship at Chatham for several years before being sold, stranding on her way to the breakers in June 1923.

HMS TRIAD

THE yacht *Triad* was built by the Caledon Shipbuilding Company and was launched on 9 November 1908. She was hired by the Admiralty in February 1915 from the National Bank of Turkey and the intention was that she be used as a Fleet Minesweeper, but instead she was employed as a Headquarters Ship. By April 1915 she was in the Dardanelles and with four destroyers guarded the Smyrna approaches to protect the landings from torpedo attacks. She was used as the Commander-in-Chief's yacht and often carried senior army officers. In early August 1915 Admiral de Robeck and General Hamilton observed the attack on Sari Bair from her bridge. She was purchased outright on 19 June and was reclassified as a Special Service Vessel, being listed as of 1202 tons. In 1919 she was the Senior Officer's Ship in the Persian Gulf and was last commissioned in Bombay in March 1932 for the same role. By then she was armed with one 12 pounder and four 3 pounder guns. She was sold in May 1933. Beyond her can be seen a *King George V* Class Battleship, the *Ajax* or *Centurion*.

HMS HUMBER

SEEN here painted in camouflage pattern and steaming through choppy seas, the *Humber* was one of the three *Mersey* Class Monitors being built for Brazil by Vickers in 1914. All three were taken over by the Admiralty in August 1914. They were designed for river work, had low freeboards and carried two 6 inch guns in a turret forward. A third 6 inch gun was added aft later, *Humber*'s extra gun being one salvaged from the battleship *Montagu* (see Vol 1 page 114). They also carried two 4.7 inch howitzers and various smaller guns were added during the war. She arrived at Dover in August 1914. While returning to Dover from Ostend, she and her sister ship the *Severn* were attacked by a submarine, but their very shallow draught of only 5 feet proved an effective counter to the torpedoes. In March 1915 *Humber* was prepared for operations in the Dardanelles, arriving there on 4th June. She was sent to Gaba Tepe immediately to deal with the Turkish guns there which were covering the approaches. In the December she had to destroy the abandoned camps at Anzac Cove. Her two sisters had, meanwhile, sunk the German cruiser *Konigsberg* in the Rufiji River. At the end of the war all three were sold, the other two being scrapped but *Humber* became a crane ship for salvage work being fitted with a 60 ton crane. The machinery used came from a variety of old ships, the turning motor from the German *Rheinland*, gun turret machinery from the German *Oldeburgh* and a generator from the sloop *Bend Or*.

Overleaf

DESTROYERS
May 1914

THE destroyers seen here are of the *Basilisk* (or G) Class. They formed the Fifth Destroyer Flotilla under the Captain(D) in the *Blenheim*, and all were tenders to *Egmont*. Vessels of this class had arrived on station in November 1913, replacing the older classes of destroyers which returned to home waters. The *Basilisks* were the first uniform class of destroyers for the Royal Navy, and they were slow (27-28 knots) but good seaboats. They were coal burning, a reversion from oil burning for fear that oil might be difficult to obtain in war, but they were the last coal burning destroyers. They were fitted with close stowing anchors and their forward gun was a single 4 inch, mounted on a deckhouse on the forecastle, a system not repeated until the V class towards the end of the war (1917). An attempt at identifying ships by using a funnel band code was tried for exercises in 1913, and pendant numbers were introduced in February 1914. Amongst this flotilla was the *Scorpion*, commanded by Lieutenant Commander A B Cunningham. The title Lieutenant Commander had become effective from 1st April 1914. The *Grasshopper* (see page 40) is on the left of the picture.

HMS GILIA

16 February 1919

THE *Gilia* was an *Anchusa* Class Sloop of the Convoy Type of the *Flower* Class. Her merchantile appearance can be compared with the plainer lines of her sister ship the *Chrysanthemum* (see page 71). It would be very hard to identify her as a warship apart from the large number of crew visible on deck. She had been launched by Barclay Curle on 15 March 1918 and was commissioned in April 1918. She was photographed here while refitting at Malta between spells of special service in the Aegean. She was sold in January 1923.

HMS WEYMOUTH
1919

THE *Weymouth* is seen here after being torpedoed off Durazzo on 2 October 1918. She had left Brindisi that day and at 1210 had been engaged by an enemy shore battery. At 1232 she was circling to port when she was fired on by the Austrian submarine U28. Two torpedo tracks were seen, one missing the starboard bow, and the other hitting her aft. She managed to steer using her main engines and returned to Brindisi. 3 men were missing, one killed and 6 were wounded. After initial repairs at Brindisi, she left there on 27 February, 1919, reaching Malta on 2nd March. Her refit lasted to May, 1920. It is interesting to compare her wartime fitted tripod foremast with the original light pole mast that can be seen in the photograph of her sister ship the *Yarmouth* (see page 20). Nameship of her class she had been launched at Elswick on 18th November 1910. Fitted with 4 shafts driven by Parsons compound reaction turbines, she was designed for 25 knots and exceeded that by a knot on trials. She spent the early years of the War in the East Indies, then served in the West Indies and off West Africa. In July 1917 she returned to Malta, wearing the broad pennant of the Commodore 8th Light Cruiser Squadron from September. In March 1919 she became a private ship again, operating in the Adriatic. After her refit and repairs of the damage seen here, she spent a commission on the South American station before being placed in reserve at the Nore. She was sold in 1928 and broken up at Blyth.

HMS SPORTIVE
16 March 1919

THE Admiralty S Class Destroyer *Sportive* is seen entering Grand Harbour, having only arrived at Malta 4 days before as part of the new Sixth Flotilla which had left Devonport on 3 March under their Captain D in the Leader *Stuart*. She left Malta in July for Sevastopol, and operated in the Black Sea until 1922. Launched at Chatham on 19 September, 1918, she had been completed in December. With a displacement of 1075 tons, this class carried three 4 inch QF Mk IV guns and six 21 inch torpedo tubes. They were also designed to carry two fixed 18 inch torpedo tubes by the break of the forecastle for short range cold firing against destroyers. Most of the class had these small tubes removed as they detracted from the seagoing qualities of the vessels, and some later vessels were never fitted with them. Their bridges were round fronted to improve seakeeping, and they had extra sheer forward. However, they suffered from excess spray on the bridge and upper deck, though some did cope with a gale whilst steaming at 24 knots. The 20 inch signal projector aft was bridge controlled by Newitt hydraulic manipulating gear, and director firing was fitted for the 4 inch guns. *Sportive* was one of the ten ships handed over to Wards in September 1936 in part payment for the liner *Majestic*, which became the training ship *Caledonia*.

HMS ROWAN
29 April 1919

THE *Rowan* had been launched in 1909 for the Laird Line Ltd, with a speed of 16 knots and Gross Tonnage of 1493. She was taken into service on 14 November 1914 as an Armed Boarding Steamer, being fitted with two 12 pounder guns and one 3 pounder. She commissioned at Glasgow on 30 November 1914 and in 1915 operated off Devonport. In June 1915 she went to Mudros via Malta, being used for carrying troops and for boarding caiques. On 18 May 1916 she was attacked by seaplanes off Mudros and suffered splinter damage. On 12 February 1917 she underwent a 3 hour bombing attack but suffered no hits, and shortly afterwards managed to avoid 28 bombs dropped at her. In April 1917 she was working off Suda Bay and Salonica and that July she was taken into use for trooping duties. That service lasted a year, during which time she took troops to Patras. She was in collision twice during that period, in November 1917 with the drifter *Clyde* and in June 1918 with the SS *Ravenizon*. In July 1918 her formal hire reverted to that of an Armed Boarding Steamer, being Chatham based but still serving in the Mediterranean. At the time this photograph was taken she was on the Aegean Ferry Service with the *Partridge II*. She paid off in August 1919 at Devonport, and was taken to Pembroke Dock for survey before being returned to trade on 15 June 1920.

HMS ANEMONE
26 March 1919

THE *Anemone* was launched on 13 May 1915 by Swan Hunter. She was one of the *Acacia* Class of Minesweeping sloops of 1200 tons and capable of $16^{1}/_{2}$ knots. Built by a variety of firms, these vessels had minor differences and they carried a variety of armament. At this time *Anemone* carries just one 3 pounder aft. Her searchlight on the bridge wing is prominent and she has semaphore signalling arms on top of the bridge. In December 1915 she had been at the evacuation of Gallipoli, Captain C Corbett directing the embarkation at Suvla from her. She had just arrived at Malta from Taranto and sailed again shortly afterwards for Gibraltar and Devonport, where she paid off on 8 May. In 1920 plans were afoot to sell her to Portugal, but the Portuguese decided she was not suitable and so her lathes were removed in 1921 and she was sold to Marple and Gillott of Saltash in September 1922.

HMS HEROIC

6 May 1919

THE *Heroic* was launched in 1906 and was built for the Belfast SS Company. With a Gross tonnage of 1869, she was capable of 18 knots. She was first taken up by the Government from 6 to 22 August 1914, for the move of the 6th Division from Ireland to England. She then reverted to trade, but was again taken up on 18 November 1914, this time to become an Armed Boarding Steamer. She was fitted with two 12 pounder guns. One can be seen on the port side forward of the bridge, whilst the other is right aft. These smaller ships were less expensive than cruisers for this often risky task. Originally she served on patrol off Queenstown, but was again used as a troopship from July 1917 to January 1918. By the Spring of 1919 she was running between Marseilles and Malta. After a refit in Malta she was in action off Ilija Bay in the Gulf of Smyrna during Greek landings to secure Western Anatolya and lost one able seaman killed and 3 officers and nine men wounded from shore fire. Shortly after this photograph was taken the *Heroic* made a further trip to Marseilles. She sailed on to Devonport to pay off, and then to Portsmouth for survey and reconditioning. She was returned to trade on 6 July 1920.

HMS CANADA
July 1919

THE Battleship *Canada* is seen entering Grand Harbour from Constantinople. After 5 days in Malta she sailed again, reaching Rosyth on 30th July. Placed in reserve for a short period, she temporarily returned to the Mediterranean with crews for ships on station. On 1st August 1920 a Chilean crew took her over at Devonport, and she became the *Almirante Latorre*, serving for another 39 years before being broken up in Japan. Originally destined for Chile she was purchased by the Royal Navy on 9 September 1914. She was being built at Elswick by Armstrong. She had been launched on 27 November 1913, but work on her and her sister ship, the *Almirante Cochrane* (see page 99) had stopped in August 1914. She was completed in September 1915. Armed with ten 14 inch guns, she was designed for 22.75 knots, her funnels being raised during building to allow her to achieve that speed without using forced draught. Speeds of 23-24 knots were claimed. She was present at the Battle of Jutland and also at the Heligoland Bight in November 1918. She had flying off platforms fitted on B and X turrets in 1918. The screw flagsmen are standing on the after flying off platform. She is also carrying a deck cargo amidships on this, her last voyage in full commission in the Royal Navy.

R. ELLIS
MALTA.

H.M.O . PEARLEAF

HMS PEARLEAF

July 1919

THE oiler *Pearleaf* was one of the 5000 ton *Leaf* Class. Built by W Gray and Co. and launched on 12 September 1916, she was completed in 1917. She was fitted with two sets of steam triple expansion engines developing 6750 horse power giving her a speed of 16 knots, but she operated at 12 knots as fuel consumption was heavy at higher speeds. Originally to have been called *Gypol*, she was renamed in 1917 to conform with the Leaf names used by other Admiralty contract tankers. During The First World War she was run by Lane and MacAndrew, she was designed to act as an escort to Atlantic convoys while carrying oil from America to the United Kingdom. It is interesting to note the flanges fitted fore and aft of the funnel making it appear upright and giving the appearance of a slower ship. She spent from 1922 to 1926 in reserve at Rosyth and was then put on charter until 1930. She was then employed on freighting duties and during the Second World War was with the China Fleet and on the Eastern Station. She was broken up at Blyth in December 1947.

HMS ASPHODEL
July 1919

THE *Asphodel* was one of 48 ships of the *Arabis* Group of the *Flower* Class of Minesweeping Sloops. This was the third order of these ships which had been designed using merchant practice where possible. This group was slightly larger than the previous two groups, but despite an extra 200 horse power, they were rated at half a knot slower than their half sisters. Six of the class were built with two 4 inch guns, whilst the remainder were completed with two 4.7 inch guns. *Asphodel*, launched on December 1915 by Henderson, had hers removed by the time of this photograph, the mounting rings can be seen forward of the foremast and aft of the mainmast. Eight of the class were completed for the French Navy. *Asphodel* was at this time employed on the Mudros-Malta-Constantinople ferry service but visited Marseilles in September, Naples in October and Smyrna in November. On 18 February 1920 she was relieved by the *Bryony* and sailed for Devonport to be placed in reserve on 20 March. She was sold to Denmark in June 1920, arrived at Harwich on 5 July, where a Danish crew joined her and she was renamed *Fylla*. She was employed on Fishery Protection duties in Icelandic waters.

SAINT MARGARET OF SCOTLAND
July 1919

THE *Saint Margaret of Scotland* had been built as the *Balantia* by Harland and Wolff, being launched in 1909 for the Royal Mail SP Company. With a Gross Tonnage of 2467 and capable of 12 knots she was 300ft 9 inches long. She was taken into service as a Hospital ship on 25 January 1916. She is seen here at buoys in Grand Harbour, having left Southampton in mid July to arrive at Malta on 22nd. She sailed on 23rd for Constantinople. She is wearing her number (19) on a board by the bridge, and is flying the red ensign. She was manned by merchant service personnel but carried naval medical staff and chaplain. Her windscoops are out to keep the messdecks cool. She returned to trade on 31 January 1920.

Overleaf

HMS CAROLINE
8 July 1919

THE *Caroline* was the nameship of the first group of C Class Cruisers, and was the first completed, being launched by Cammell Laird in September 1914 and completed in December 1914. Originally given a mixed armament, with two single 6 inch guns aft and with eight single 4 inch guns forward and along her sides, by 1919 she had been re-armed with four single 6 inch guns as can be seen in this view. A pair of torpedo tubes was fitted on each side amidships and she carries single AA guns each side of the bridge at forecastle level. She achieved 29.07 knots at full power during her acceptance trials. She served with the Grand Fleet during the war and was present at the Battle of Jutland. After the war she sailed for the East Indies, and it was on her passage out there that this photograph was taken. She arrived at Malta on 6 July, and sailed again on 8 July for Port Said, Aden and Bombay. She paid off in 1922 and became the RNVR Drill Ship at Belfast in April 1924, having all her guns removed except for one 3 inch and one 12 pounder, and a deckhouse containing a 6 inch in one corner and a single 3 inch in each of the other corners. She still remains at Belfast as a commissioned ship.

HMS HONEYSUCKLE
19 July 1919

THE *Honeysuckle* was a *Flower* Class Sloop of the *Acacia* Group, one of the first 24 ordered in December 1914. She was launched by Lobnitz on 29 April 1915 and was very similar to her sisters *Anemone* (see page 60) and *Sunflower* (see page 73), although there were slight variations as builders made their mark. *Honeysuckle* has a longer area of accommodation under her funnels. She served most of her active career in the Mediterranean. Captain A D Boyle, who was in charge of the evacuation of the Anzac area of the Dardanelles embarked in her in December 1915, his own ship, the *Bacchante* (see page 9) being in reserve at Kephalo at that time. Here she is seen lying in Malta where she spent two weeks prior to departing for Suda Bay and Mudros on the ferry service which also took in visits to Constantinople. There was quite a variety in this service as she also visited Corfu and Taranto. Towards the end of the year she left Malta for good, arriving at Devonport on 11 December to be paid off to care and maintenance. She was sold in September 1922.

HMS EMPRESS
16 August 1919

THE *Empress* had been a fast cross Channel packet, launched in 1907 by Denny and was requisitioned in 1914. Turbine driven she was capable of 21 knots. She was converted into a seaplane carrier by Chatham Dockyard and fitted to take four to six seaplanes. A canvas hangar was fitted aft with the capacity for four aircraft, together with a crane for lifting the aircraft out to the water and for recovering them. She was first used in home waters, her aircraft raiding Cuxhaven in December 1914. The raid took place in a fog and during the confusion caused in the roadstead the German battlecruiser *Von der Tann* collided with a cruiser and both were badly damaged. In Mid 1916 she operated off Palestine, the Sinai Peninsula and the Yemen in operations against the Turks. Later her aircraft were employed on anti-submarine duties. She is seen here leaving Malta for Mudros and Constantinople, having paid off on 12 June and recommissioned on 14 June. In September she was at Odessa but returned to Malta on 4 October to transfer her stores to the *Ark Royal* (see page 92) prior to her return to Sheerness on 25 October for a refit before being returned to her owners in November 1919. She was resold in 1923 and was broken up in 1933.

HMS HUSSAR
26 August 1919

THE Torpedo Gunboat *Hussar* was launched in 1894 at Devonport Dockyard and another photograph of her appears in Volume 1 (page 93). She had become the Admiral's yacht on the Mediterranean Station in 1907 but in 1909 had her forecastle gun replaced for patrol work. She served in the Dardanelles campaign and later in the Aegean and in 1919 reverted to the duties of yacht and despatch vessel. She is seen here leaving harbour with the Commander-in-Chief embarked. This photograph was probably taken when the *Hussar* was sailing for visits to Constantinople, Marseilles, Piraeus, Mudros and Novorossisk. The tug astern of her is the *Restive* (see page 77 under *Tobago*). The *Hussar* was paid off on 28 July 1920 at Malta and was sold locally to Mr L Gatt. She was relieved by the *Surprise*, ex *Razsvet*, which had been renamed in 1920 and was sold in 1923.

HMS CHRYSANTHEMUM
August 1919

THE *Chrysanthemum* was one of the second (*Anchusa*) Group of "Convoy Type" *Flower* Class Sloops. Their design had been influenced by the early successes of the Q ships, and they looked like merchant ships, all with one funnel, some with two masts, others with one, and with decks either open or canvassed over. The *Chrysanthemum*, launched by Armstrong, Elswick on 10 November 1917, presents a very smart appearance with her flush deck and single mast. Her port side 4 inch gun is visible just aft of her accommodation ladder, whilst a single 12 pounder can be seen right aft under her awning, where a defensively armed tramp ship would carry a gun. In July 1919 the *Chrysanthemum* had been employed on the Gibraltar to Malta ferry service. This service was discontinued on 18 July, and it was planned that she relieve the *Bryony* as the flagship to Rear Admiral Egypt. But this was cancelled, and she sailed from Malta on 8 August for Devonport where she was fitted out for target towing work and for photography, returning to Malta on 17 December 1919. In August 1937 she was allocated to the London Division of the Reserves, arriving to join the *President* (ex *Saxifrage*, a sister ship) on 12 May 1939. She remained there until 1987, when she was sold for conversion to a Museum ship. A sister ship was the *Gilia* (see page 56).

HMS ALACRITY
September 1919

THE yacht *Margarita* had been renamed *Semiramis*, and later, when purchased by a Russian Princess, the *Mlada*. She was taken over by the Admiralty as the Armed Boarding Steamer *Mlada* from 16 September 1918, and was taken over entirely in March 1919. She was commissioned on 7 August 1919 as the *Alacrity*, a traditional name for despatch vessels. She sailed from Devonport on 26 August with Vice Admiral Sir Alexander L Duff KCB embarked en route to be Commander-in-Chief China Station. After stopping for 4 days at Gibraltar, she arrived at Malta on the morning of 6 September. She is seen here in Grand Harbour with a large awning over her after deck by the foot of the mainmast and with her boats marked with the Admiral's flag. She has her admiralty pattern anchor secured to the bulwark just aft of her graceful clipper bow, with its scrollwork and figurehead. She left Malta on 10 September, calling at Port Said, Aden, Colombo and Penang before reaching Singapore on 9 October. At Singapore she transferred her flag to the cruiser *Hawkins* before sailing on to Hong Kong. She was paid off in September 1922 and was sold in 1924.

HMS SUNFLOWER
October 1919

THE *Sunflower* was a Fleet Sweeping Sloop of the *Acacia* group of the *Flower* Class. These vessels were designed to make as much use as possible of merchant vessel practices so that as many builders could be employed in their construction as possible. The average building time for these vessels was 25 weeks, and many were used as convoy escorts. They had a triple hull at the bow to withstand collision or mine damage and had a flat keel from forefoot to sternpost. They had a wide turning circle and were lively, but safe, in a seaway. *Sunflower* was built by Henderson and launched on 28 May 1915, being commissioned at Glasgow on 5 July 1915. For the first few years she operated off Queenstown helping to salve the *Terpsichore* in Long Island Sound in May 1916. In 1917 she moved to Scapa Flow, and in April attacked a submarine with depth charges. She was employed minesweeping off Scapa in 1917 and off Grantham in 1918. She first arrived at Malta on 17 September 1919 on her way to Constantinople. She returned to Malta on 17 October, remaining until 30th when she sailed for Portsmouth, and thence Southampton where she was to be laid up. On 23 October she was sold to the Rangoon Port Commission and was renamed *Lanbya*.

HMS ENGADINE

12 October 1919

THE *Engadine* had been built in 1911 by Denny as a fast cross Channel packet. She was requisitioned on 11 August 1914 and was converted at Chatham Dockyard to carry four seaplanes in a large hangar built on her stern. Commissioned on 13 August 1914, her aircraft took part in the Cuxhaven raid in December 1914 with those of the *Empress* (see page 69). She operated with the First Light Cruiser Squadron in May 1916 in raids to lure the German High Seas Fleet to sea. She was operating with the Battle Cruiser force on 31 May for reconnaissance and spotting but her reports had no effect on the action. The next day she met the crippled cruiser *Warrior* and took her in tow, but finally had to rescue the *Warrior's* ship's company before she sank. She was deployed to the Mediterranean in early 1918 and was photographed just after arriving from Constantinople. Her square hangar, which replaced an original canvas one, can be seen here, together with the AA guns fitted on its forward end. She carries two guns right aft as well. She sailed on 18 October and arrived at the Nore on 1 November and started preparations at Chatham for her return to commercial service. She was returned to her owners in December 1919, restarting work in July 1920. She was resold several times and was finally lost as the *Corrigidor* in December 1941 by hitting a mine in Manilla bay.

HMS CORNFLOWER
28 November 1920

THE *Cornflower* was a sister ship of the *Ashphodel* (see page 64) and comparisons can be made to see the different appearance of ships of the same group of the *Flower* Class. Some of this class were built in under 19 weeks, the average being under 6 months. They fulfilled the need for a better and more numerous class of minesweepers which could also be used as general utility ships for carrying baggage and liberty-men for the Fleet. She lacks a large mainmast and had more of the midships accommodation plated in. Launched by Barclay Curle on 30 March 1916 she had just arrived from Jeddah for a refit period when this photograph was taken. The refit completed on 27 December, when she sailed again for Port Said and Jeddah. Beyond her can be seen the battleship *Iron Duke*, visiting Malta from Constantinople, and there is a cruiser on the left of the photograph. She was still carrying her single 4 inch guns forward and aft, and by the after gun there were some 3 pounders. In 1935 she became the RNVR Drill Ship at Hong Kong, and was sold in 1940, being renamed *Tai Hing*. In September 1940 she was bought back and given her original name. She was sunk by air attack at Hong Kong on 15 December 1941.

HMS CARDIFF
28 October 1920

THE *Cardiff* is shown here sailing for Gibraltar where she was to refit and recommission, hence the paying off pennant streaming out from her foremast. Her relief crew arrived at Gibraltar in the battleship *Conqueror* and she recommissioned on 15 December, sailing from Gibraltar on 20 December and arriving at Malta 3 days later. A day afterwards she became the Flagship of the Third Light cruiser Squadron. The Admiral was Vice Admiral Sir George P W Hope KCMG CB, who had shifted his flag temporarily to the *Centaur*. He was relieved in January by Rear Admiral Sir Reginald Y Tyrwhitt Bt KCB DSO DCL. In October 1921 the *Cardiff* went to Galatz to embark ex King Karl and his wife Zita and to take them to Madeira.

   Cardiff had been originally named *Caprice*, but her name was altered before she was launched in April 1917 by Fairfield. Only five feet longer than the first C class group, the *Caroline* group, this group (the *Ceres* Group) carried an extra six inch gun and were two knots faster, and also gained additional accommodation with the extra forward superstructure. She was damaged in the Heligoland Bight action on 17 November 1917, being hit three times by gunfire and narrowly missed by a torpedo. She was selected to lead the High Seas Fleet to their surrender in November 1918 and later served in the Baltic supporting the Latvians and Estonians against the Bolsheviks. She served world wide between the wars and spent the Second World War in home waters, firstly on the Northern patrol and then as a gunnery training ship. She was sold in January 1946.

HMS TOBAGO
13 December 1920

THE *Tobago* is seen being brought into Grand Harbour by the tugs *Cracker* and *Restive*. She had been mined on 12 November in the Black Sea but suffered no casualties. She was towed to Malta by the battleship *Centurion*, starting out from Constantinople on 9 December. A Thornycroft built S Class Destroyer, launched on 15 July 1918, it is interesting to compare her with her half sister, the *Sportive* (see page 58). She has a wider forefunnel, and taller after funnel, the forecastle gun is mounted on a bandstand whilst the break of the forecastle is led further aft to give more protection amidships. Marginally longer, beamier and with a higher freeboard than the standard S Class, the Thornycroft craft had 2000 more shaft horse power and *Tobago* reached 38.21 knots on trials. She was broken up at Malta in February 1922. The tugs were both of the *Dromedary* Class, their coal fired steam reciprocating engines developing 1250 horse power which could drive them at 10 knots. The *Cracker* had been launched in 1900 and served at Malta from 1911 and later was at Sheerness before being broken up in 1956. The *Restive* had been launched as the *Restless* in 1902 by Day and Summers. She had been renamed in 1916 whilst at Malta, and was sold in 1938.

Overleaf

HMS TEMERAIRE
8 October 1920

THE *Temeraire* was a Battleship of the *Bellerophon* Class, and had been launched at Devonport on 24 August 1907. Her completion had been delayed until May 1909 through a strike by employees of Engineering contractors. She served with the Home Fleet before the war and became part of the Grand Fleet, being present at Jutland. She had minor modifications to her secondary armament arrangements and control tops, and was fitted with a single anti-aircraft gun during the war, but overall her appearance altered little, compare her with the photograph of her sister *Bellerophon* taken before the war (see page 32). In March 1915 she had attempted to ram the German submarine U29 but the *Dreadnought* hit the submarine first. In October, 1918 she had transferred to the Eastern Mediterranean to re-inforce Admiral Gough-Calthorpe's force after the surrender of Turkey. After a few months in reserve, she commissioned on 24 September 1919 as a Cadets' Training Ship under Captain LAB Donaldson CMG. She is seen here arriving at Malta from Gibraltar, having sailed from Rosyth on 14 September. She should have visited Algiers but had only stopped off that port for mail as the bubonic plague had been reported there. On 26 October she left for Palermo, Palma, Gibraltar, Lisbon, Torbay and Portsmouth. Cadets can be seen working on the forecastle. She paid off in April 1921 and was sold that December, being broken up at Dover in 1922.

HMS BENBOW
20 December 1920

THE *Benbow* was an *Iron Duke* Class battleship built by Beardmore and completed in October 1914. These were the last coal fired battle-ships, carrying over 3000 tons at full load. She served with the Grand Fleet during the war, then went to the Mediterranean in 1919. She was present at the start of the operations against the Turks off the Southern coast of the Sea of Marmara in June 1920 with her sisters *Iron Duke* and *Marlborough*. She is seen here returning from Constantinople. She had transferred the Flag of the Rear Admiral Commanding the 4th Battle Squadron (Rear Admiral Sir Richard Webb KCMG CB) to the *Emperor of India* the day before arriving. She returned to Constantinople, sailing from Malta on 23 January 1921, and joined the *Centurion* until March.

In 1926 she joined the Atlantic Fleet and paid off in 1929. She was sold for breaking up in March 1931.

H.M.S. PEGASUS

R.Ellis
MALTA

HMS PEGASUS
1 February 1921

THE seaplane carrier (later seaplane tender) *Pegasus* was laid down at John Brown's yard as the *Stockholm* and was purchased on 27 February 1917. She was launched on 9 June and renamed on 28 August. She had been ordered for the Great Eastern Railways for their continental passenger service and was turbine driven with a speed of 20.25 knots. She had a flying off platform forward where the aircraft were handled by two derricks on the twin foremast. Right aft was a large hangar which also had cranes for lifting aircraft out and onboard. She operated with the Grand Fleet in 1917 and 1918, and in 1919 worked in the White Sea and then went to the Mediterranean. She is seen here on trials. She had arrived at Malta in November 1920 from Constantinople to undergo a refit. She is pictured here after that refit which completed on 15 January 1921. She sailed for Smyrna on 12 February and remained in the Mediterranean that year, recommissioning at Malta in December. Unlike her contemporaries, she was retained after the war and did not return to commercial work. After she had been sold for breaking up in August 1931, her name was taken by the seaplane carrier *Ark Royal*, releasing that name for the new aircraft carrier which was laid down in 1935.

H.M.S. VINDICTIVE

R ELLis
MALTA

HMS VINDICTIVE
February 1921

THE cruiser *Vindictive* had been laid down as the *Cavendish* and was launched under that name in January 1918 by Harland and Wolff. Her name was changed in June 1918 to commemorate the cruiser of Zeebrugge fame. She was completed as an aircraft carrier, retaining some of her cruiser armament, having 7.5 inch guns at A and Y positions and also amidships on each side. B gun deck became a flying off platform with windbreaking pallisades and derricks, and a large flight deck for flying off aircraft was fitted abaft the funnels. It was planned that she would be an 'alighting ship' for the recovery of aircraft flown from other cruisers, but she was completed too late to be tried operationally. She ran aground during operations in the Baltic in 1919. Strangely two others (*Raleigh* and *Effingham*) of this class of 5 were lost through grounding. This photograph was taken after her repairs and just prior to her paying off to reserve in March 1921, with paying off pennant flying on a windy day.

Laid up for a period, though used for trooping duties, she was reconstructed at Chatham as a cruiser in 1923-1925, but retained her forward hangar. In 1936 she was converted to a Training Ship with a token armament and a single funnel and was then made into a repair ship at the start of the war. She took part in the Norwegian campaign and served in the South Atlantic and Mediterranean before being paid off in 1945 and sold in 1946.

HMS CONCORD
21 March 1921

ORIGINALLY one of the *Canterbury* Class of C Class cruisers, the first group with only two funnels, she and her sister the *Centaur* were modified while building to carry a uniform armament of five 6 inch guns. These two were, in fact a re-order, to use a large amount of machinery that had been ordered for two Turkish scout cruisers. *Concord* was completed at Elswick in December 1916. She had a designed speed of 27 knots on 4 shafts. Her bridge was well forward to allow an extra 6 inch gun to be added between the bridge and the funnels and so she was heavy forward and wet in a seaway. Her AA guns can be seen mounted fore and aft of the searchlight platform amidships. Later ships had them sited to give better arcs of fire. She was photographed here sailing for Gibraltar for a 42 day refit after waiting in Malta for six weeks to take the Secretary of State for the Colonies from Brindisi to Egypt. This task was cancelled. After her refit she cruised in the Eastern Mediterranean prior to recommissioning at Malta on 1 August. In 1925 she visited Australia and China before returning to the Mediterranean in 1926. She was placed in reserve later that year and partly disarmed. She was used for trooping in 1928 and then was attached to the Portsmouth Signal School before paying off in 1933 and being sold in September 1935.

HMS BLENHEIM
4 April 1921

The *Blake* Class cruiser *Blenheim* had been completed in 1892 with a main armament of two 9.2 inch guns and ten 6 inch guns. However, she was converted to be a destroyer depot ship in 1906 and her armament was reduced to four 6 inch guns and four 4 inch guns, and later to three 4 inch guns. At first she was employed as a depot ship in home waters, but moved to the Mediterranean in 1913. In August 1914 she took her destroyers to the Dardanelles and whilst there became the parent for sixteen destroyers, six submarines and 21 minesweepers. In October 1917 she returned to Malta with three divisions of destroyers and in 1919 went back to Constantinople. In April 1921 a relief crew was brought out to Malta in the *Undaunted*. The *Blenheim* had been there since September 1920. She recommissioned at Malta on 14 April 1921 and sailed for the Black Sea on 6 July. In August, the crew of the destroyer depot ship *Diligence* exchanged ships with the crew of the *Blenheim*, and then *Blenheim* sailed for the United Kingdom. She called at Devonport on 29 September and then at Sheerness before arriving at Harwich on 6 October, where she paid off and recommissioned with the crew of her sister ship, the *Blake*. She became the depot ship for minesweepers at Harwich and later at Sheerness, paying off in 1925 and being sold the next year.

H.M.S. KING GEORGE V.

R. ELLIS
MALTA.

HMS KING GEORGE V
1921

THE battleship *King George V* is seen leaving Grand Harbour for Constantinople. Her appearance had not altered very much from when she was completed at Portsmouth Dockyard in November 1912. The main difference, comparing her with the pre war photographs of her sisters *Ajax* (page 46) and *Audacious* (page 44), are the removal of her torpedo nets and booms, which gives her a clean appearance. Her bridgework has been enlarged, her searchlights re-arranged, and the forecastle gun ports have been plated over. She has two anti-aircraft guns on her quarterdeck. *King George V* alone was given a full tripod mast to support the enlarged control top, the others of the class having short struts to support the foremast. A flying off platform had been fitted on B turret. She had been fitted with anti-rolling tanks when built, but as they were not very successful they were converted to extra fuel tanks. After leaving the Mediterranean in 1923, she paid off at Devonport and then recommissioned with a special complement as a gunnery firing ship, carrying out firings off Scotland, the Channel coast and also Shoeburyness. In November 1923 she became a tender to the *Impregnable* and was sold in 1926.

HMS CERES
18 May 1921

THE *Ceres* was launched on the Clyde in March 1917 and completed on 1 June 1917. She was the first C Class cruiser with the superfiring gun in B position. She joined the Sixth Light Cruiser Squadron on completion, and was at the Heligoland Bight action on 17 November 1917. She transferred to the Third Light Cruiser squadron in the Mediterranean in 1919 and landed troops at the Dardanelles in July 1920. She was photographed as she sailed for Tunis, the first time Tunisia had been visited by a British Warship since it had become a protectorate of France in 1881. Her balanced profile gives an impression of speed. Designed for 29 knots on two shafts, she achieved 29.1 knots on trials and 29.5 knots for 4 hours during overload trials. Between the wars she served in the Mediterranean when not in reserve. She returned to the Mediterranean in 1940 and in 1941 took part in operations against the Italians in Eritrea, Abyssinia and E. Somaliland, bombarding coastal defences, supply dumps and concentrations of enemy troops. She stayed with the Eastern Fleet until 1943, when she returned to home waters. She was placed in reserve as an accommodation ship, after being one of the escorting ships for the Normandy landings. She was sold in April 1946 and was broken up at Blyth in July 1946, when her name was taken into use by the RN Supply School at Wetherby.

HMS LUCIA AND SUBMARINES
October 1922

THE *Lucia* is seen here in Dockyard Creek with the submarines L25 and L52 alongside her, whilst L22 and L24 are lying astern. The *Lucia* was built by Furness Withy and Co in 1907 as the Hamburg-Amerika liner *Spreewald*. She was captured off Trinidad on 12 September 1914 by the cruiser *Berwick* whilst she was supporting the German cruiser *Karlsruhe*. She was converted to a submarine depot ship on the Clyde in 1916, and served until 1946, when she was sold, finally being broken up at La Spezia in 1951. This photograph was taken while the *Lucia* was part of the Atlantic Fleet, but visiting the Mediterranean for exercises. L24 was launched in 1919 by Vickers and was lost in January 1924 when in collision with the battleship *Resolution* off Portland. Here she is temporarily attached to the Second Submarine Flotilla. L22 and L25 were also launched in 1919 by Vickers and were broken up in Newport in 1935. L52 was launched in 1918 by Armstrong and was broken up at Pembroke Dock in 1935. The L Class were a development of the H Class, slightly larger at 890 tons to the H Class's 364-500 tons, they carried a gun, had more torpedo tubes and had a higher surface speed. 27 were built and a further 8 were cancelled at the end of the war. The L50 class were slightly larger again at 960 tons and carried a second 4 inch gun. Six of these were built and 20 were cancelled. One of the cancelled vessels was completed as a salvage vessel and the materials for two others were used in the construction of two Jugoslav submarines, one of which (the *Tara* ex *Nebojsca*) served under Allied control in the Second World War.

HMS EMPEROR OF INDIA
1923

LAID down as the *Delhi* by Vickers in May 1912, her name was changed in October 1913, one month before she was launched. Completed in November 1914, she was the only ship in which the Loyal toast was 'Gentlemen, the King Emperor', and the crown on her ensign staff rested on a cushion. One of the four *Iron Duke* Class battleships, she had a main armament of ten 13.5 inch guns, the last class fitted with them, and had a secondary armament of twelve 6 inch guns, an improvement over the 4 inch of previous classes. The after 6 inch guns proved to be mounted too low to be workable in any seaway and so were removed to the forward shelterdeck where they had a wide arc of fire. She served with the Grand Fleet during the war and joined the Mediterranean Fleet in 1919. She spent the first part of 1923 in the Black Sea and returned to Malta in June and stood by in case she was required to assist at the Etna disaster. In October she underwent a four month docking and repair period. Flying off platforms can be seen fitted on her B and Q turrets and her foretop had been enlarged since she was built. After serving her last three years with the Atlantic Fleet, she was paid off in 1929 and was used as a gunnery target, being sunk on 1 July 1931, raised and sold for breaking up at Rosyth.

HMS ROYAL SOVEREIGN
4 February 1923

LAUNCHED at Portsmouth Dockyard on 29 April 1915, the *Royal Sovereign* was completed in May 1916. She served with the Grand Fleet during the First World War, but in 1920 was in the Mediterranean as part of the force landing 8000 Greek troops to occupy Panderma in the Sea of Marmara. Here she is photographed arriving at Malta from Chatham prior to sailing two days later for the Dardanelles. She returned to the United Kingdom in October 1923. This view shows how her secondary armament of 6 inch guns were placed further aft than in the *Queen Elizabeth* class. She has low anti-torpedo bulges fitted. Her overall appearance is very sturdy, with a small, compact superstructure dominated by the two powerful twin 15 inch turrets forward and aft. A flying off platform can be seen on the top of B turret. She was little modernised before the Second World War, where she was employed on convoy escort work. She served in the Mediterranean and Eastern Fleets prior to being transferred to Russia as the *Archangelsk* in May 1944. She was returned in February 1949 and was sold for breaking up shortly afterwards.

───────

Overleaf

HMS LUCIA, ADAMANT AND SUBMARINES
1926

THE *Lucia* is seen here with part of the Mediterranean bases Second Submarine Flotilla which comprised five of the L50 Class of submarines. The vessel in the foreground, looking very like a yacht with her clipper bow and bowsprit is the *Adamant*, built in 1911 and which operated as a submarine depot ship with the *Lucia*. The Second Flotilla had arrived at Malta on 8 February 1925 from the Atlantic Fleet. The *Adamant* was sold in 1932, although her sister ship, the *Alecto*, served until 1949. The three submarines closest to the *Lucia* have Asdic domes on their conning towers. This Asdic was the type 113C, which was fitted in four of the class in 1925, making them the first to use Asdic operationally. Sea trials had been carried out in submarine H22 in 1922 using set type 113, while in the same year set type 114 had been fitted in the destroyer *Rocket*. The crow's nest fitted on the foremast of the *Lucia* is a reminder that radar had not yet been conceived, whilst on the jetty are two horse drawn gharries, the then equivalent of modern taxis and which are still retained for their tourist value. The *Lucia* paid off in December 1926, the Flotilla being taken under the wing of *Maidstone* at Devonport in November, 1926.

H.M.S. ARK ROYAL

R. ELLIS
MPGA.

HMS ARK ROYAL
7 April 1923

THE seaplane carrier *Ark Royal* is pictured here entering Grand Harbour after a period at Constantinople as an aircraft transport and depot ship. She had a mixed RN/RAF crew on deck. After a docking from 9 to 18 April she returned to Constantinople and the Chanak area. In the September she returned to Chatham to pay off for reserve. Laid down by the Blyth Ship Building Company as an oiler, she had been purchased while building in May 1914, four months before her launch, and was completed as a mobile seaplane base to carry four aircraft. Her single shaft drove her at 11 knots, too slow for any ordinary deck launch, and the plan was to lower the aircraft to the sea using the cranes which also lifted the aircraft out of and into her hangar. The aircraft would take off and land on the sea. However, a 130 foot long launching platform was built on the bows and some aircraft could be launched on trolleys. She arrived at the Dardanelles in February 1915, but she was withdrawn in the June as she was too slow to avoid torpedo attacks. In 1923 she was converted to a depot ship and between the wars carried out trials of catapults and Hein Mat experiments. She was renamed *Pegasus* in December 1934 to release her old name for the new aircraft carrier. At the outbreak of the Second World War she was in reserve but quickly commissioned as an aircraft transport. In 1941 she was converted to be a fighter catapult ship and served on Atlantic Convoys until 1944, when she was used as an accommodation ship. She was sold in October 1946, being broken up at Grays in April 1950.

HMS REVENGE
26 MARCH 1923

THE *Revenge* is seen here entering Malta from Chanak flying the Flag of Rear Admiral A A M Duff CB, Commanding the First Battle Squadron. She sailed two days later for the United Kingdom for repairs, remaining in Home Waters for the rest of the year. From this angle the distinctive curve of the break from the forecastle to the six inch gundeck can be seen. Also, the *Revenge* alone of her class had a stern-walk. She had low anti-torpedo bulges, whilst *Royal Oak* and *Ramillies* were later given very high bulges. Originally to have been called *Renown*, she was completed by Vickers Armstrong at Barrow in March 1916 and was present at Jutland, becoming the Flagship of Vice Admiral Sir Cecil Burney KCB KCMG, Second in Command of the Grand Fleet when the *Marlborough*, his original Flagship, was hit by a torpedo. In the Second World War she was employed escorting convoys and in October 1940 bombarded Cherbourg. She stood by in home waters in case *Scharnhorst* and *Gneisenau* came out of Brest and was sailed from Halifax during the *Bismarck* chase. After a period with the Eastern Fleet she returned to the United Kingdom in September 1943 and became the Naval Base at Gareloch. She was taken to Inverkeithing for breaking up in September 1948.

HMS COVENTRY
25 April 1927

THE *Coventry* had been laid down as the *Corsair* in August 1916. She was launched as the *Coventry* by Swan Hunter on 6 July 1917 and was completed in February 1918. Her group of the C Class introduced the second 6 inch gun into a superfiring position (B position) forward of the bridge. Bridge, boilers and funnels had been placed slightly further aft. This gave a far wider arc of fire and also improved the seakeeping qualities with a better weight distribution. In 1920 she had been the Headquarters ship for the Naval Inter-Allied Disarmament Commission. On 8 March 1923 she suffered a torpedo explosion whilst at Malta in which two men died. She was Flagship of the Rear Admiral (Destroyers) Mediterranean from 1923 to 1928, and again, after a refit, in 1930 to 1934. She was seen here wearing the Flag of Rear Admiral the Hon H Meade CB CVO DSO, sailing for exercises prior to leaving for Corfu and the Aegean. The gun mounted high ashore on Dragutt Point appears to be fitted forward of her B gun as she leaves Sliema Creek. In 1935-1936 she was given a prototype conversion to an anti-aircraft ship, being fitted with ten single 4 inch guns and two multiple machine guns. She was damaged in Ofotfjord in the Norwegian campaign in 1940. Late in the year she again returned to the Mediterranean, and was damaged by a torpedo off Sidi Barani in December 1940 and by a near miss off Crete in May 1941. Her gunlayer was awarded a Victoria Cross. She was repaired at Bombay from October 1941 to June 1942 but in September 1942 was lost off Tobruk trying to cover the withdrawal of *Zulu* from attempts to rescue the *Sikh*. She was hit by four large bombs and had to be sunk by torpedoes from the *Zulu* (see page 141).

HM SUBMARINE X1
April 1927

THIS very unusual submarine was built at Chatham Dockyard and was the only Royal Naval warship laid down after World War I to be scrapped before the Second World War. Launched on 16 June 1923, by Mrs Kiddle, wife of the Admiral Superintendent, she sailed from Chatham for trials on 3 June 1924, but was not formally commissioned until 25 September 1925. With a displacement of 2780 tons, she was the Royal Navy's largest submarine prior to the introduction of nuclear propelled vessels. She was armed with two twin 5.2 inch guns and six torpedo tubes. Her main engine diesels were built at Chatham and developed 6000 shaft horse power giving her a speed of $19^1/_2$ knots. She had, however, an electrical overdrive to give her 26 knots. She had two auxiliary diesels for battery charging taken from the German merchant submarine *Deutschland*. She sailed for the Mediterranean in January 1927 with the cruiser *Conquest* and the submarines L18, L26 and K26. They arrived at Malta on 7 April, and X1 left on 6 July for the Aegean after repairs. She refitted in Malta from September until March 1928. She suffered an explosion in No 1 battery room when in dock in July 1929, and after another explosion in January 1931 was reduced to one third crew at Chatham in February 1931. Placed in reserve in that September, five years later it was decided to sell her, and she was one of the ships given to Wards in December 1936 in exchange for the *Majestic*.

HMS CALYPSO
23 May 1927

THE *Calypso* was one of the *Caledon* Class, which were slightly larger than their predecessors with a longer forecastle to improve their sea-keeping. The straight raked bow that was introduced with this class is clearly visible in this photograph. They were also the first to carry deck mounted torpedo tubes instead of submerged tubes, being fitted with eight in twin mountings. She was completed in June 1917 by Hawthorn Leslie and served with the Grand Fleet during the First World War. During the Heligoland Bight action in November 1917 she was hit on the bridge and everyone in the conning tower was killed. In 1918 she served in the Baltic and captured the Bolshevik destroyers *Avtroil* and *Spartak* off Reval in December 1918. She then served in the Mediterranean from 1919 to 1928 and again from 1929 to 1932 after a refit. She was photographed here sailing for Gibraltar and then to Sheerness for docking. She paid off in the August and recommissioned for the Mediterranean again. At the outbreak of the Second World War she was on the Home Station, and intercepted the German *Minden* in September 1939 and captured the *Konsul Hendrik Fisser* off the Faroes in November 1939. She sailed for the Mediterranean in 1940 and was sunk by the Italian submarine *Bagnolini* on 12 June 1940 south of Crete with the loss of 39 of her crew.

HMS HERMES
October 1927

THE *Hermes* had commissioned at Portsmouth in June 1925 for the Mediterranean but was temporarily detached to the China Station in 1926. She was photographed here on 15 October 1927 on her way back to Portsmouth, where she recommissioned prior to returning to the Far East. The *Hermes* was the first aircraft carrier to be built as such from the keel up, being laid down at Elswick in January 1918. She was launched on 11 September 1919 and completed in February 1924. She had two propeller shafts and could steam at 25 knots. She was armed with 5.5 inch guns along her sides and with 4 inch AA guns by the island. She could carry 20 aircraft in her hangar, which was aft. The aircraft were raised to the flight deck by an electrical lift fitted on the quarterdeck. She proved a very steady ship with little rolling at sea and had a good size flight deck (600 by 90 feet). It is interesting to note the low position in which her anchors were housed. At the outbreak of war she served in the Atlantic and her aircraft attacked the French battleship *Richelieu* at Dakar in July 1940. In 1941 she was used on convoy duties and supported troops in operations against Italian East Africa. In April 1942 she was sent to Trincomalee to prepare for the assault on Madagascar, but was attacked by Japanese aircraft off Ceylon. She was hit by 40 bombs in 10 minutes and sunk. 600 survivors were rescued by a nearby Hospital Ship.

HMS CALEDON
Autumn 1927

THE *Caledon* was launched on 25 November 1916 and completed in March 1917 at Cammell Laird's. Originally fitted with five single 6 inch guns, the second gun mounted between the bridge and the forefunnel had a very restricted arc of fire. She served with the First Light Cruiser Squadron in the First World War, and was hit by a 12 inch shell when in action in the Heligoland Bight in November 1917. Ordinary Seaman T H Carless manning the forward 6 inch gun was awarded a posthumous Victoria Cross for this action. She later served in the Baltic before joining the Third Cruiser Squadron in the Mediterranean in 1927. She commissioned at Chatham in August 1927 and sailed for Malta. In January 1928 she was in collision with an Italian oiler in the Doro Channel and her bows were badly damaged. She had to be towed stern first to Malta and repairs took until the end of April. At the time of this photograph she had a revolving aircraft platform just forward of her midship searchlight platform. This had replaced a flying off ramp on her forecastle and hangar which had been built into the starboard side of her bridge in 1917. Her searchlight platform amidships was a trial type with experimental 24 inch projectors fitted in 1924. She was in home waters on the outbreak of war and served there, in the Mediterranean and East Indies before being converted to an AA cruiser in 1942-1943. This was a major refit, with the bridge being moved aft so that two twin 4 inch guns could be fitted forward. She then served in the Mediterranean. She was sold for breaking up in 1948.

HMS EAGLE
26 October 1927

THE *Eagle* had been laid down in 1913 as the Chilean battleship *Santiago*, later the *Almirante Cochrane*. Her sister became *HMS Canada* (see page 62), but *Eagle* was purchased in 1917 and completed for trials in April 1920 and was commissioned in February 1924 as an aircraft carrier. At first she had a single funnel. A forefunnel was added soon afterwards together with tripod mast and a control top. She carried 21 aircraft and also had nine 6 inch guns mounted along her sides, three of which can be seen in this view. Single 4 inch AA guns were mounted fore and aft of the bridge structure, with smaller guns around the funnels. She introduced the island to aircraft carriers. Her full length flight deck and workshops fitted on her battleship hull, which rode high out of the water, made her an impressive vessel. She was pictured here arriving at Malta from Suda Bay and Venice for a three month refit. When the war started she was on the China Station. She was at Calabria in July 1940, and a month later her aircraft sank the Italian submarine *Iride* and a depot ship and destroyer. In October they bombed and mined Tobruk. Her aircraft were lent for the Taranto raid. In 1941 her aircraft sank or put out of action several destroyers in the Red Sea, caught the blockade runner *Elbe* and helped capture the tanker *Lothringen*. In 1942 she helped to supply Malta with Spitfires and supported the convoys to the island. During Operation Pedestal, on 11 August 1942, she was torpedoed by U73. Four torpedoes hit her and she sank in 8 minutes, but 929 of her 1160 officers and men were rescued.

HMS DANAE
1927

THE *Danae* was a D Class Cruiser of 4650 tons, launched by Armstrong on 26 June 1918. She was unusual in that she was the only one of the class not fitted with either a trawler bow or an aircraft hangar under the bridge. (Compare her with the *Delhi*, page 119). Here seen just after commissioning for the Mediterranean as part of the Second Division of the First Cruiser Squadron. The sailors below B gun are heaving the lead in the chains by the carley float. Her triple 21 inch torpedo tubes can be seen in the waist level with the funnels and the after searchlight platform. These ships carried a heavy armament of twelve torpedo tubes. She served worldwide between the wars and during the Second World War operated mainly in Eastern waters. In 1944 she took part in the Normandy landings and in the following October she was lent to the Polish Navy, being renamed the *Conrad*, serving with them until September 1946. She was sold in 1948. Beyond her can be seen the Second Division of the First battle Squadron comprising the R Class battleships *Royal Oak* (Flagship) on the right, *Resolution* (with funnel cap) and *Ramillies* (on the left) as they lie off the entrance to Grand Harbour.

FIRST BATTLE SQUADRON
1927

THE battleship *Warspite* is seen leading her sister ships *Queen Elizabeth* and *Valiant* out of Grand Harbour past St Elmo Point during the autumn of 1927. The *Queen Elizabeth* has just returned to the Mediterranean after a major refit, during which her two funnels were trunked into one and anti-torpedo bulges were fitted. *Warspite* was the first of the class to receive this refit, whilst the *Valiant* still retains her original two funnelled appearance, not being refitted until 1929. From this angle the plates over the position where the after 6 inch guns were to have been mounted in the *Valiant* can be seen. Only the *Queen Elizabeth* carried these guns as experience in the *Iron Duke* Class had already shown that they were too exposed to be worked at sea. The *Warspite* is wearing the flag of Vice Admiral J D (Joe) Kelly CB, Vice Admiral Commanding the First Battle Squadron. She hit an uncharted rock in the Aegean on 12 July 1928, and returned to the United Kingdom. The captain of the *Warspite* from December 1927 was Captain J F Somerville DSO, who commanded Force H in the Mediterranean during the war.

Overleaf

HM SUBMARINE L21
November 1927

THE L Class Submarine L21 was launched by Vickers on 11 October 1919 and was sold to Dalmuir for breaking up in February 1939, and so did not take part in either World War. She was one of the second group of the class, built with six torpedo tubes, two more than the first group of eight boats of the class, and she mounted a 4 inch gun at the forward end of her conning tower. It was not until the late 1920s that the next class of submarines was built, and so the L class were the mainstay of the submarine force for the ten years that followed the Great War. Here the L21 is seen leaving Marsamxett Harbour for exercises on a blustery November morning, with the cruiser *Cardiff* (see page 76) lying further down Sliema Creek wearing the flag of the Rear Admiral Commanding the Third Cruiser Squadron.

HMS WREN
2 February 1928

THE Modified W Class destroyer *Wren* was photographed arriving at Malta from Brindisi and Valona. Beyond the breakwater can be seen two of her half sisters, the *Volunteer* (over her bow), another Modified W of the same group, whilst the *Witch* (seen over *Wren's* torpedo tubes) is of the Third Modified W Group. *Witch* has a wider forefunnel and taller after funnel. The *Witch* was, incidentally, the last V & W in commission in June 1946. The *Wren* had been launched by Yarrow on 11 November 1919 and was completed at Pembroke Dockyard in January 1923. The Modified W Class were armed with four 4.7 inch guns and two sets of triple torpedo tubes. Her anti-aircraft armament comprised two single two pounders mounted en echelon abaft the after funnel. *Wren* was distinctive in having no caps to her funnel tops. These destroyers were built with a limited endurance of 4 to 5 days, having no refrigerators. They were planned to cruise around the United Kingdom, drawing provisions from ashore when required. *Wren* was lost whilst on an anti invasion patrol off Aldeburgh on 27 July 1940. She went to the aid of some minesweeping trawlers which were under air attack and was sunk by the aircraft.

HMS WORCESTER

6 February 1928

THE *Worcester* was a Modified W Class Destroyer of the second group, launched by Whites on 24 October 1919 and completed at Portsmouth Dockyard in September 1922. This class had larger forefunnels and thin after funnels. She was seen here entering Grand Harbour after a visit to Zante and Dragamesti. She sailed again on 16 March for Pollensa Bay and then Gibraltar. She was relieved in the Fourth Destroyer Flotilla by the *Amazon* and was then placed in reserve in Malta, her crew taking the *Woolston* (a Thornycroft W Class Destroyer) from reserve in Malta to the United Kingdom in February 1930. *Worcester* was damaged off Dunkirk in May 1940. In March 1941 she helped drive off E boats from an East Coast convoy. In February 1942 she was in the 16th Flotilla at Harwich when the *Scharnhorst* and *Gneisenau* broke out of Brest. With 5 other destroyers she crossed a minefield to reach an attacking position and she closed to within 3000 yards of the German ships before being stopped and swept by gunfire. She was set on fire and lost 4 killed, but the crew managed to put the fires out and bring her back to harbour despite attacks by aircraft of both sides. Later that year she took part in Russian convoys, and in 1943 helped drive off an attack by 32 E boats on a convoy off Cromer. She sank one E boat with a direct hit and damaged another. In December 1943 she was damaged when a mine exploded under her stern. Not repaired, she became an accommodation ship and was renamed *Yeoman* in June 1945. She was sold in February 1947. Two biplanes are visible above her mainmast.

THE RAMESES DANCE BAND

THE larger the ship, the broader the choice of entertainments as a general rule. The *Rameses* Dance Band, seen here in the same hall as the *Sentinel* Entertainers (see page 51), represented one group from the battleship *Ramillies*, whose badge can be seen at the bottom of the drum on the left of the picture. In their evening dress it is hard to tell who they were, but the range of instruments indicates that they were probably a talented group. The *Ramillies*, a *Revenge* Class Battleship (see page 122), completed in 1917 and carried some 900 men. This could have been a detachment of Royal Marines, and possibly part of a Royal Marine Band. However, it is remarkable how talented sailors are, and this group could just as well have been seamen, signalmen, stewards or stokers, or even members of the Wardroom. On the other hand, it may well have been a mixture of personnel. Most of them look as though they take their music seriously, but two seem relaxed enough to smile.

RAOB - 'GROVE HOUSE' LODGE
1928

APART from bands, sports and entertainments, other groups were also formed to bring men together and help pass the time usefully. Here is a three score strong group of 'Buffaloes', showing a wide variety of rates, ranks and branches, with some civilian members. The front rows are bedecked with sashes and medals, whilst the others wear their best uniforms for the occasion. In the rear row is a rangetaker, and in the row in front of that is a stores or writer rating wearing the star badge on his right arm to indicate his trade. At this time Officers' stewards and cooks wore a plain disc known as 'the plate', and it was not until 1933 that they adopted the 'star' badge too. There seem to be many members of the torpedo branch present, including a Petty Officer sitting in the front row.

HMS WOLSEY
November 1932

THE *Wolsey* was one of a pair of Thornycroft W Class Destroyers, with a distinctive large after funnel. They were armed with the smaller 4 inch guns but carried the triple, instead of twin, torpedo tubes. She had been launched on 16 March 1918 and was a special, being the fastest of the V and W Class destroyers with a speed of 38.183 knots on trials. Whilst on the China station in 1927 she had four tons of protective plating fitted on the bridge and around A and Y guns and her pom poms, landing her torpedo warheads and other equipment to compensate for the topweight. She was given a 'Wair' conversion in December 1939, which left her with a twin 4 inch gun in A and X position and also a modified bridge. Her torpedo tubes were landed. Thus equipped she arrived at Dunkirk on 31 May 1940 to act as a wireless link. She was damaged whilst at Dunkirk, but survived the war and was one of the ships that entered Stavanger in May 1945 when Norway was released from German control. Named after the Cardinal, her motto was 'To the last penny! tis the King's' (from Shakespeare's Henry VIII). Sold in March 1947, after 29 years' service, she gave the value for money indicated by her motto.

HMS TITANIA AND SUBMARINES
December 1929

THE *Titania* was purchased in 1915 when she was building on the Clyde and was completed as a Submarine Depot Ship. In 1921 she took a flotilla of L Class Submarines out to the China Station and remained there until 1929. This picture was taken during her return passage to the United Kingdom. She arrived at Malta on 30 December, and has the Fourth Submarine Flotilla of L Class Submarines berthed on each side of her. L20, launched in 1918 by Vickers and sold to Cashmore in 1935, is seen half dived, possibly to allow work to be carried out under the waterline aft. L3, launched by Vickers in 1917 and sold to Charlestown in 1930, and L19, launched by Vickers in 1919 and broken up at Pembroke Dock in 1937, are inboard of her. The L class were capable of 17 knots on the surface and $10^{1}/_{2}$ knots submerged, the earlier vessels of the class having four torpedo tubes, the later vessels six. The *Titania* was sold to Metal Industries at Faslane in 1948.

HMS SUSSEX
22 April 1932

THE *Sussex* was one of the *London* Group of the *County* Class, being launched by Hawthorn Leslie on 22 February 1928. She completed on 19 March 1929 and sailed to join the First Cruiser Squadron in the Mediterranean. She is seen here entering harbour after visiting Palma and Algiers. She has an aircraft amidships and her high sides without bulges can be seen clearly. She left Malta again on 14 May with the Commander-in-Chief embarked taking him to meet the First Lord at Mentone. In 1934 she exchanged duties with the *Australia* and was operating off Australia until 1936. She was little modified before the war, four extra single 4 inch AA guns being added. She intercepted the German blockade runner *Watussi* in the South Atlantic in 1939. While in dock at Greenock in September 1940 she was bombed and partly capsized. Repairs took until August 1942. She sank the German tanker *Hohenfriedburg* off the Azores in February 1943. The tanker was being escorted by 3 submarines, one of which fired at *Sussex* but missed. At that time she was on passage to the Eastern Fleet, where she remained until 1944. After a refit in Sheerness she returned to the East Indies and in operations off Malaya shot down two kamikaze aircraft, one crashing fifty yards from the ship and causing slight hull damage. She was the Flagship for the return to Singapore in September 1945 and the surrender there was signed onboard. In November 1945 she covered the landings in Indonesia. She was sold in January 1950.

HMS REGENT
30 March 1933

THE *Regent*, an R Class submarine of 1475 tons, had been launched on 11 June 1930 by Vickers Armstrong at Barrow. She commissioned at Barrow on 20 September 1930. She was photographed when returning from Bona and Pollensa for a docking at Malta. She was then part of the First Submarine Flotilla, operating from the depot ship *Cyclops*, with Captain S1, Captain R W Blacklock DSC Royal Navy in the Leader *Douglas*. She was fitted with six bow torpedo tubes, and two stern tubes, and carried an open 4 inch gun forward of the conning tower. After her docking she spent a further two months away from Malta visiting Corfu, Brioni, Venice, Biograd and Kotor. In April 1935 she went to Hong Kong to become part of the 4th Submarine Flotilla. She returned to the Mediterranean during the war, sailing from Malta for the last time on 11 April 1943 for a patrol in the Adriatic en route to Beirut. She is known to have attacked a convoy 5 miles north east of Monopoli on 18 April and it is believed that she hit a mine, for bodies were found on 1 May that had been a week in the sea. Both her sisters lost in the war (*Rainbow* and *Regulus*) were sunk in the same area in 1940. The fourth member of the class, the *Rover*, survived the war to be broken up at Durban in July 1946.

HMS RESOLUTION

November 1933

THE *Resolution* had recommissioned at Devonport with a Portsmouth crew on 7 September 1933, and sailed for Malta via Gibraltar under Captain J H D Cunningham MVO Royal Navy. She towed the mooring vessel *Buffalo* to Gibraltar and arrived at Malta on 10 November. *Resolution* had been completed in December 1916 by Palmers, and subsequently had been given low anti-torpedo bulges (compare with the high bulges in *Ramillies*, page 122). She has a clinker screen on her funnel, fitted in 1922. The bridge and gunnery control positions suffered badly from smoke in a following wind and it is surprising that it was not until 1938 that others of the class were so fitted. She was also fitted with a trial anti-aircraft mounting on the starboard side of her upper deck abreast the funnel. This was a twin 4 inch gun in a turret, a design used later in the twin 4.5 inch guns fitted in the fleet aircraft carriers and also the modernised *Queen Elizabeth*, *Valiant* and *Renown*. In October 1939 she took bullion to Halifax and afterwards escorted convoys in the Atlantic. She was damaged by bombing off Norway in May 1940, and more seriously damaged when torpedoed off Dakar in September 1940. After repairs at Philadelphia, she joined the Eastern Fleet and undertook more convoy escort duties. She returned to Britain in September 1943, and was used as a training ship before being sold in 1948. Beyond her can be seen the Battleship *Queen Elizabeth* (see page 126).

HMS TERROR
2 November 1933

THE *Terror* was a 7200 ton monitor built by Harland and Wolff at Belfast. She was completed in August 1916, just 10 months after being laid down. Her main armament was the twin 15 inch gun turret forward, but her secondary armament of four single 4 inch each side with a single 3 inch anti aircraft gun aft of the 4 inch can be seen clearly in this view. Also to be seen on the upper deck are five cars, for at this time she had commissioned in July 1933, and was on passage to Singapore to become the Base Ship there. During the First World War she had been hit by three torpedoes. Two hit her bow and caused much damage, whilst the third struck her bulge and did none. She served on the Dover Patrol and after the war was attached to the Gunnery School at Portsmouth. She was at Singapore from 15 January 1934 to 29 January 1940, when she returned to the Mediterranean. She joined the Inshore Squadron which was formed in January 1941 to supply and support the Army in North Africa. She was bombed by Italian aircraft off Derna on 22 February 1941 and sank on 23rd.

Overleaf

HMS BOREAS
1934

THE Destroyer *Boreas* was completed in February 1931 by Palmers. She had commissioned in October 1933 for the Mediterranean and her First Lieutenant was Lieutenant G B Roope (see HMS *Glowworm* page 132). The A and B Classes introduced quadruple torpedo tubes and full shields to the 4.7 inch guns. They were designed for 35 knots which they achieved with ease, the *Arrow* achieving 36.7 knots for six hours on trials. On trials *Boreas* reached 35.78 knots. She is carrying a propeller on a board on the front of her bridge, whether this is in allusion to her name or her speed is uncertain, though it was not her official badge. Beyond her can be seen the *Vindictive* (see page 82) whilst over her stern her sister the *Bulldog* can be seen entering French Creek. In 1939 she was an attendant destroyer to the *Ark Royal* and *Furious* and in November 1942 took part in Operation Torch. During the war she had her after funnel reduced, after torpedo tubes and B and Y gun removed. She was lent to the Greek Navy in April 1944 and renamed *Salamis*. She was returned in September 1951 and was sold for breaking up in November 1951.

HMS DECOY
April 1933

LAUNCHED by Thornycroft at Woolston on 7 June 1932, Decoy was completed in April 1933, completing to full complement on 4th at Devonport. She is seen here shortly afterwards arriving at Malta showing from her fore-funnel that she was a Divisional Leader, and from her after funnel that she was in the First Flotilla. This class were fitted with high speed sweeps and has a single 3 inch AA gun between the funnels. They were a repeat of the C Class, four of which were cancelled as a gesture of unilateral disarmament and the other four of which were purchased by the Canadian Navy in 1937/8. The C Class had introduced depth charge throwers to the armament of 'between the wars' destroyers. She was the only one of her class that survived the war. She was in the Mediterranean at the start, being present at Calabria, the operations off Greece and Crete and later Libya. She was damaged during the evacuation of Crete. She was modified as an Atlantic escort in 1942, fitted with radar, her after torpedo tubes removed and Y gun taken off to allow more depth charges to be carried. She was transferred to the Royal Canadian Navy in 1943 and renamed *Kootenay*. As such she helped sink *U678*, *U621* and *U984* in 1944. She was sold in January 1946 for breaking up in Canada.

HMS DAINTY

23 April 1934

THE D Class destroyer *Dainty* was photographed steaming stern first into harbour. This was often done in Malta to avoid turning inside the harbour. She had been built by Fairfield and launched in May 1932, completing in January 1933. She cost £229,378 and achieved 36.11 knots on trials. It was found that she had a wire rope around her propeller and her port shaft was damaged. On first arriving at Malta she had to dock as she had damaged her hull under water during heavy weather. After a first commission in the Mediterranean she sailed for the China Station and remained there until 1939. She returned to the Mediterranean when the war started and was present at the bombardment of Bardia in June 1940. That month she and the *Ilex* sank two Italian submarines off Crete. She was at Calabria in July 1940 and escorted convoys to Malta before being sunk by dive bombers off Tobruk on 24 February 1941.

HMS DELHI
1934

The *Delhi*, a D Class Cruiser built by Armstrong, Wallsend, launched on 23 August 1918, was completed in June 1919. The D Class had a large armament of six 6 inch guns – one being mounted between the bridge and forefunnel, as can be seen in this view – and twelve torpedo tubes. They had a speed of 29 knots and later ships of the class, including *Delhi*, had a trawler bow fitted to improve their seakeeping qualities. Her revolving flying off platform for aircraft is visible just forward of the amidships searchlight platform, and her anti aircraft gun abaft X 6 inch mounting is pointing skywards. She appears to be preparing for sea, with her cable veered to allow the quarterdeck party to prepare their wires at the after buoy, and the accommodation ladder has been raised. However, the very small jack she is wearing might indicate preparations for a heavy blow coming on, as her lower boom is still rigged. She served in the Mediterranean from 1925 to 1928 and from 1932 to 1938. In the Second World War she gained six battle honours there. During the war she was refitted with American 5 inch guns and directors. She was badly damaged at Split in February 1945, repairs were abandoned and she was broken up at Newport in 1948.

Opposite

HMS FURIOUS
28 July 1934

ONE of three heavy cruisers to be converted to aircraft carriers, the *Furious* was converted before her first commission in 1917, being fitted with a flight deck forward and carrying a single 18 inch gun aft. In November 1917 she was modified to carry aircraft forward and aft, the after turret being replaced by a second hangar and a deck running from her single funnel to the end of the hangar. This deck was 300 feet long and fifty feet wide. With her mainmast removed and her secondary armament of 5.5 inch guns resited, she was fully an aircraft carrier. However, when she joined the Fleet in March 1918 it was found that the flight deck was dangerous because of turbulence, and shortly afterwards she was laid up. In 1921-1923 she was rebuilt. She was seen here in her fully converted guise, carrying 33 aircraft and with ten 5.5 inch guns along her sides. She could steam at 30 knots, her funnel being removed and the smoke ducted aft, hence the black painted stern. Her conning position could be lowered for flying operations. She was later given a small island structure and her AA armament was improved by the addition of six twin 4 inch guns. She was active throughout the Second World War, ferrying aircraft to Malta in 1941 and escorting convoys to the island in 1942. Her last operation before being placed in reserve was in September 1944 covering a minelaying operation off Norway. She was sold in January 1948.

HMS DURBAN
15 August 1934

THE cruiser *Durban* was a fine sight as she entered Grand Harbour from the Aegean. Four days after arrival she hoisted the Flag of the Rear Admiral Third Cruiser Squadron, Rear Admiral H J S Brownrigg CB DSO, who transferred from the *Delhi*. Launched by Scotts on 29 May 1919, she was completed at Devonport Dockyard in October 1921. She was in the second group of the D Class and had a trawl bow fitted to improve her seakeeping qualities. This class carried six 6 inch guns and a heavy armament of twelve torpedo tubes. Her two port triple torpedo tubes can be seen amidships in this view. She carried two single 4 inch AA guns by her funnels and a third can be seen right aft of X gun beyond the Royal Marine guard. For a period she had carried a revolving flying off platform amidships forward of the search-light and rangefinder platform, but this had been removed by the time this photograph was taken. In 1939 she was in reserve at Portsmouth, but soon commissioned and served on the South Atlantic Station and then the China Station. She was damaged by bombs during the evacuation of Singapore in February 1942 and repairs took six months. She then rejoined the Eastern Fleet, returning home in 1944 to be used as a breakwater off Normandy during the invasion.

HMS RESOURCE

19 October 1934

THE *Resource* was a Fleet repair Ship of 12,300 tons displacement, launched by Vickers Armstrong, Barrow on 27 November 1928. Her armament comprised four single 4 inch anti aircraft guns, two of which can be seen on her quarterdeck, whilst the other pair was mounted on the forecastle. She was fitted with a very large crane amidships, only part of which can be seen in this view, and she carried two smaller cranes in the well amidships. Her bridge was forward of the well deck and had a small gunnery director on it. She was here entering Malta having been to Portsmouth to recommission. In 1937 she was placed in reserve and also acted as an accommodation ship for submarine crews whilst the Depot Ship *Cyclops* was detached as a depot ship for Flying boats at Arzeu. At the outbreak of war she was with the Mediterranean Fleet helping it to be self reliant in view of the insecurity of the base at Malta and the lack of facilities at Alexandria. She was moved through the Suez Canal in July 1942 when Alexandria was threatened by the German advance. She was sold in February 1954.

HMS RAMILLIES
7 November 1934

The *Ramillies* is seen here entering Grand Harbour on her return to the Mediterranean having completed to full complement at Sheerness on 11 September for further service with the First Battle Squadron. In June 1935 she was at Sheerness to exchange ship's companies with the *Valiant*, who was going to the Mediterranean whilst *Ramillies* went into reserve. She was the last of her class to enter service, as she damaged her rudder during launching at Dalmuir in November 1913 and had to be repaired by Cammell Laird at Liverpool. She was the first battleship completed with anti-torpedo bulges, which were enlarged in her 1924-1927 refit. The addition of bulges reduced her speed only slightly. She carried a catapult on X turret served by a special crane. Although this class was given minor refits, they never received the large scale modernisations that other old capital ships had. *Ramillies* escorted convoys for the first few years of the war, and joined the Eastern Fleet in 1942. She was Admiral Syfret's flagship for the capture of Diego Suarez. She was damaged by a Japanese midget submarine whilst there. She took part in the Normandy landings and then those in Southern France. She was sold in 1949 after 32 years service. One of her guns is at the entrance to the Imperial War Museum.

Opposite

PRINCE GEORGE'S WEDDING
29 November 1934

THESE two scenes show ships illuminated for the celebrations following the marriage of Prince George, Duke of Kent to Princess Marina, daughter of Prince and Princess Nicholas of Greece, at Westminster Abbey. The single ship is the *County* Class Cruiser *Devonshire*, completed at Devonport Dockyard in March 1929 and at this time serving on her second Mediterranean commission. She had been plagued by bad luck during her early commissions, including an explosion in a turret. The silver replica of Drake's drum which had been presented to the ship on commissioning was landed, and this seemed to break the run of accidents. The other photograph shows the Battleship *Queen Elizabeth* with the Commander-in-Chief's flag illuminated. Around her are moored the *Revenge* Class Battleships *Ramillies* (on the left with the tripod mainmast), *Resolution*, *Revenge* and *Royal Sovereign* (one of which is not visible in this photograph). Beyond the *Ramillies* can be seen the Aircraft Carrier *Hermes* (see page 97). The *Hermes* had arrived two days before from Portsmouth, and sailed again the day after this photograph was taken on her way out to the China Station. She arrived at Singapore on Boxing Day.

HMS CYCLOPS AND SUBMARINES
April 1935

THE Submarine Depot Ships *Cyclops* was purchased whilst building as the *Indrabarah*. She was launched by James Laing & Co of Sunderland in October 1905. The *Cyclops* had two single 4 inch guns painted black on her forecastle. Alongside her were the R class submarines *Regent* and *Regulus*, both of whom had been in the Mediterranean for a period. The *Rover* was the submarine in third position out, and she had arrived from a refit at Devonport. All three were to sail on 1 May for the China Station. The fourth submarine was either the *Otway* or the *Oxley*. The two outboard submarines were the *Shark* and *Sealion*, the former having commissioned on 5 October 1934 and the latter on 22 September 1934. Both arrived at Malta on 12 April. The *Cyclops* was to take six submarines with her to the Jubilee review at Spithead in July, including *Otway, Oxley, Shark* and *Sealion. Regent* and *Regulus* were both lost in the Mediterranean during the war, but the *Rover* survived to be broken up at Durban in 1946. *Oxley* was torpedoed by accident by the *Triton* in September 1939 and the *Otway* was broken up in 1945. Both these O class vessels had been in the Royal Australian Navy from 1927 to 1931. The *Shark* was scuttled in the Skaggerak in July 1940 after a two hour fight with aircraft. The *Sealion* was later commanded by Cdr B Bryant (later Rear Admiral B Bryant CBE DSO (2 bars) DSC) and became an anti-submarine target in March 1945. The *Cyclops* outlasted them all, being broken up at Newport in 1947.

HMAS AUSTRALIA
17 May 1935

THE *Australia* was completed by John Brown in April 1928 and after trials sailed for Australia. In 1935 she exchanged duties with the *Sussex*. She left Brisbane on 6 December 1934, flying the standard of HRH the Duke of Gloucester. After reaching Portsmouth she sailed for Malta and seen here on arrival. She returned to Devonport in June to have her catapult installation completed and then attended the Jubilee Review in July. She returned to Fremantle on 2 August 1936. She did not receive the large modernisation that her RN contemporaries received before the war, but was given extra anti aircraft guns in 1940. Later she was fitted with tripod masts and X turret was removed. She spent most of the war in Eastern waters, though she was present at the abortive attack on Dakar in July 1940, replacing the *Fiji* which had been torpedoed. She was present at the battle of Coral Sea and at Savo Island, where she missed the night action. She then covered landings in the Pacific. On 21 October 1944 a Japanese aircraft crashed onboard and she had to be taken in tow. In January 1945, at Lingayen Gulf, she was with the Fire Support Group when she was hit by four kamikaze aircraft. She was repaired at Devonport and Sydney. She was sold in January 1955 and was broken up at Barrow.

Overleaf

HMS QUEEN ELIZABETH
24 August 1936

The battleship *Queen Elizabeth* was photographed arriving from Gibraltar and Barcelona. Her captain at this time was Captain E L S King, who returned to the Mediterranean as a Rear Admiral flying his flag in the *Naiad* during the campaign for Crete in 1941. The *Queen Elizabeth* had been launched at Portsmouth on 16 October 1913, and was completed in January 1915. She was sent to the Mediterranean to calibrate her 15 inch guns in relative safety and became involved in the Dardanelles operations. Returning to the Grand Fleet, she was Admiral Beatty's Flagship at the surrender of the German High Seas Fleet in 1918. By 1936 she had already been refitted with a single funnel, and a year later she was taken in hand for a far greater modernisation, improving her main and secondary armament and fitting an aircraft catapult amidships and a new bridge structure. New high pressure boilers reduced her weight in compensation whilst maintaining her speed. Her refit completed in 1941 and she served in the Mediterranean at Crete and was later damaged in a human torpedo attack at Alexandria in December 1941. She was repaired in Norfolk, Virginia, and then joined the Eastern Fleet, supporting air strikes and carrying out bombardments. She was placed in reserve in 1946, and was sold in 1948.

HMS PENELOPE
27 April 1937

THE cruiser *Penelope* is seen here leaving Grand Harbour for the Spanish coast to search for survivors reported to be in an open boat after their ship had been torpedoed by an unknown submarine fifty miles off Barcelona. The *Penelope* had been in Malta for repairs, as she had lost a topmast while rolling excessively off the North Western coast of Sardinia. Completed by Harland and Wolff on 13 November 1936, she was one of the *Arethusa* Class armed with six 6 inch guns. *Penelope* and *Aurora* unlike their earlier sisters were built with four twin 4 inch AA guns mounted aft of the after funnel. *Penelope* also carried an extra director abaft her mainmast. Designed to be manoeuvrable and to be able to accelerate quickly to lead destroyers, welding was used extensively to save weight. During the Norwegian campaign she was hit by a bomb and the next day grounded off Fleinver. Repairs took 15 months. She and *Aurora* then joined Force K. On 8 November 1941 they sank a complete convoy off Cape Spartivento and just over a week later sank another convoy West of Crete. In December, however both were damaged by mines and the cruiser *Neptune* and destroyer *Kandahar* were lost. In March 1942 she was damaged by bombing and whilst undergoing temporary repairs in Malta used 6500 rounds of 4 inch ammunition, and she had to sail for Gibraltar with empty magazines. Known as "The Shadow" while with Force K, she became known as "*HMS Pepperpot*" as a result of her numerous holes after the severe bombing. She returned to the Mediterranean after repairs in America, but was lost with 415 of her crew when torpedoed off Anzio on 18 February 1944. The destroyer in the background was the *Glowworm* (see page 132).

HMS BERWICK
24 June 1937

The *County* Class cruiser *Berwick* was entering Grand Harbour from the China Station where she had been serving in the Fifth Cruiser Squadron. Four days later she sailed for Gibraltar escorting the submarines *Shark* and *Salmon*. She reached Devonport on 6 July, where she reduced to a navigation party. She arrived at Sheerness on 10 July and paid off for a refit which lasted to late 1938. One of the first group of the *County* Class, she had been launched in March 1926 by Fairfield, and was completed in February 1928. She was the only Royal Naval ship of the class fitted with Brown Curtis turbines, the remainder having Parsons turbines, and she averaged 32 1/2 knots on trials. Her funnels had been raised just after building, and in 1932 she had a catapult fitted at Devonport. The catapult can be seen just aft of the funnels. In 1934 quadruple machine guns were fitted each side of the foremast. Her refit in 1937 was on a larger scale. Her bridge was modified and a hangar was fitted aft. She was given four twin 4 inch AA guns and multiple pom poms. At the start of the war she intercepted blockade runners and in 1940 was damaged by Italian gunfire at Cape Spartivento. A month later she was again damaged, this time by German gunfire from the *Admiral Hipper* while defending a convoy North West of the Azores. She was repaired at Rosyth and Portsmouth. During the war she had her hangar and aircraft removed and radar fitted instead, and she was given tripod masts. She helped cover Arctic convoys and also carrier attacks on Norway. In May 1945 she was at Trondheim to take over and transfer U boats. She was then used for trooping duties to the Far East before being laid up. She was sold in June 1948.

HMS MALAYA
July 1937

THE *Malaya* was a *Queen Elizabeth* Class battleship presented as a gift to the Royal Navy by the Federated Malay States. Completed in February 1916 at Elswick she suffered heavy casualties at the Battle of Jutland, where she received 7 hits by large shells. She had a major refit when her two funnels were trunked into one in 1927-1929 and later was given an updated AA armament. Her twin 4 inch can be seen mounted just above the after guns of the 6 inch battery. She was seen here entering Grand Harbour after a day's steaming, having set out for Haifa but then returning as her visit was not required. Instead she sailed in mid August for a cruise of the Eastern Mediterranean. Her machinery was not modernised during her second refit in 1934-1936 and so she was not as up to date as her sisters when the war started. She took part in the action off Calabria in July 1940 and in 1941 was on convoy escort work when her presence deterred attacks by German surface ships. On 20 March 1941 she was torpedoed off Cape Verde and had to scatter her convoy whilst she made for Trinidad. She returned to the Mediterranean until 1943 when the *King George V* Class relieved her. She then was on the Clyde in care and maintenance but commissioned as a bombardment ship in June 1944 before becoming a tender to *HMS Vernon*. She was sold in 1948.

HMS LONDON
24 August 1937

THE *London* is seen following the *Hood* and the *Repulse* out of Grand Harbour at the start of the autumn cruise to Argostoli, Venice, Patras, Ierissos and Alexandria. She was flagship of Vice Admiral C E Kennedy-Purvis CB Vice Admiral Commanding the First Cruiser Squadron. The other ships in the Squadron were the *Shropshire, Sussex* and *Devonshire*, all four being of the second (or *London* Group) of the *County* Class. This group had internal bulges rather than external ones, and this improved their speed by half a knot. Their bridges were 15 feet further aft to give the forward turrets better arcs of fire. At this time *London* carried four single 4 inch anti-aircraft guns each side of the funnels. This class had been designed to carry aircraft, but the planes were not fitted until after their completion. In 1939, *London* underwent a major reconstruction, with an enlarged bridge and only two funnels. None of the others of her class received such a radical facelift. She served in the Atlantic, intercepting three German supply vessels in June 1941. Shortly afterwards she escorted convoy QP1 from Russia, having carried British and American supply missions, led by Lord Beaverbrook and Mr Harriman, there. She later served in the East Indies, the surrender of the Japanese forces in Sumatra being signed onboard by Vice Admiral Hirose on 31 August 1945. In April 1949 she was badly damaged in an attempt to rescue the *Amethyst* on the Yangtse, losing 70 killed. She paid off in 1949 and was broken up the next year.

HMS GLOWWORM
24 August 1938

THE *Glowworm* was a G Class Destroyer, launched by Thornycroft on 22 July 1935 and first commissioned in January 1936. *Glowworm* was unusual in that she was testing the quintuple torpedo tubes that were introduced with the I Class. The whole class had tripod mainmasts, which had been tried in two of the E Class. The tripod mast avoided the need for stays, and stays would have interferred with the mine rails with which this class were fitted. Otherwise she carried the standard four single 4.7 inch guns as main armament together with two quadruple machine guns between the funnels. She returned to Portsmouth to recommission on 25 July 1938 and her new Commanding Officer was Lieutenant Commander G B Roope. She returned to Malta on 9 August and in September escorted the *Strathnaver* and *Vasna* to Alexandria before going on to Aden with the *Arethusa* and the Second Destroyer Division. By April 1940 she was in home waters and was part of the screen for the battlecruiser *Renown* for Operation Wilfred, the laying of mines in Norwegian waters. She left the screen to search for a man overboard and lost contact with the force. On the morning of 8 April 1940 she ran into the German forces heading north to invade Norway and managed to ram the *Admiral Hipper* before being sunk. Lieutenant Commander Roope was awarded a posthumous Victoria Cross once details of the action became known.

HMS NELSON
14 February 1938

THE *Nelson*, wearing the Flag of Admiral Sir Roger Backhouse GCB GCVO GCMG Commander-in-Chief Home Fleet, is seen entering Grand Harbour with the *Queen Elizabeth* (see page 126) beyond wearing the Flag of Admiral Sir Dudley Pound GCVO KCB, Commander-in-Chief Mediterranean. The *Nelson* was arriving from Palma and sailed a week later for Oran and Gibraltar before returning to home waters. The *Nelson* was one of two battleships completed after the First World War whose design was unusual in having all their nine 16 inch guns forward. This was to reduce the length of the armoured belt, saving weight to keep the vessels within the international rules, and they became known as Cherry Tree Ships, as they were 'cut down by Washington'. Each 16 inch shell weighed 2461 pounds, and with the guns having a 40 degree elevation they had a 35,000 yard range. The engine rooms were forward of the boilers. They were not fast, their two shafts giving them 23 knots, but they did have an improved secondary armament, with the 6 inch guns in twin turrets, which had a 60 degree elevation and so could be used for AA work. *Nelson* was mined at Loch Ewe in December 1939 and repairs took 8 months. She took part in several Malta convoys and bombardments at Sicily, Salerno and Normandy, where she was again mined. She also served in the Far East and was at Singapore for the official surrender there. She returned home in late 1945 and was sold in 1948 after a period as a training ship.

HMS GIPSY
24 August 1938

THE *Gipsy* was a G Class Destroyer of 1335 tons launched by Fairfield on 7 November 1935. She was completed in February 1936. She recommissioned at Devonport on 22 July 1938 before returning to the Mediterranean as part of the First Flotilla. The Flotilla marking was the single red band on her after funnel. At this time she was commanded by Lieutenant Commander R G Onslow, later Admiral Sir Richard George Onslow KCB DSO (and 3 bars) DL who served in destroyers from 1926 to the end of 1945. In September 1938 she sailed for Alexandria and Famagusta for exercises. In 1939 she was in home waters and on 21 November she rescued the crew of a German minelaying aircraft which had crashed off the East Coast. She put to sea after landing them at Harwich and hit a mine laid by the aircraft whose crew she had just rescued. She was badly damaged, beached, and found to be beyond repair.

HMS ARK ROYAL
19 January 1939

THE *Ark Royal* had been built at Cammell Laird's, and was completed on 16 November 1938. She incorporated all the lessons of flying operations to date, with a proper island, two aircraft hangars, two catapults, a speed of just over 30 knots and a good anti-aircraft armament of sixteen dual purpose 4.5 inch guns. She was just arriving at Malta for a four day visit prior to sailing to Alexandria and then Gibraltar for exercises. Some of her mixed crew of RN-RAF personnel had been joined by a Royal Marine band on her flight deck. She was flying the Flag of Vice Admiral G C C Boyle CB CMG, Vice Admiral Aircraft Carriers. She was back at Portsmouth by March, a measure of how little time she had to work up as the threat of war loomed. She lived up to her designers expectations, achieving 31.75 knots on trials. Her flight deck was six times as long as the previous *Ark Royal* (see page 92) and over twice as wide and was served by two electrically powered lifts. One of her Skua aircraft shot down the first German aircraft to fall to the British on 26 September whilst she was covering the return of the damaged submarine *Spearfish* from Norwegian waters. It is hard to highlight her very active career, but perhaps her aircraft strike on the *Bismarck* is best remembered. She was torpedoed on 13 November 1941 when returning from a successful operation to transfer Hurricanes and Blenheims to Malta. She had only one man killed, but lost power and after 14 hours sank when only thirty miles from Gibraltar.

HMS WARSPITE
13 January 1938

THE *Queen Elizabeth* Class Battleship *Warspite* is seen entering harbour for the first time after her second major refit in her career. Launched at Devonport in November 1913, she suffered severe damage at the Battle of Jutland. In 1924-1926 she had received a major refit when her two funnels had been trunked into one (see page 101). However, in 1934, with her hull 21 years old, she was given a major refit which included reboilering to maintain her speed, whilst her main armament of 15 inch guns had its elevation increased from 20 to 30 thus improving its range to 30,000 yards. Eight 4 inch anti-aircraft guns were mounted together with eight barrelled pom poms (amidships) and multiple machine guns (on B and X turrets) to improve her air defences, and the whole bridge structure was rebuilt, with the abolition of the old control top. Unlike her sisters, who were modernised after her, she retained her port and starboard 6 inch guns and batteries, although the forward and after guns of the battery were removed, and the flare was moved further aft allowing the forecastle deck to be widened. This refit cost £2,362,000 almost as much as her original cost of £2,524,148. She was one of the most heavily engaged ships in the Second World War, when her modernisation paid full dividends. She was sold in 1946, being wrecked off Cornwall on her way to the breakers.

HMS HOOD – SHIP'S COMPANY
1 January 1939

The *Hood* was temporarily in the Mediterranean from October 1936 until January 1939. She had taken the Flag of the Battlecruiser Squadron from the *Barham*, and Rear Admiral Geoffrey Layton CB DSO, who had relieved Vice Admiral Andrew B Cunningham CB DSO in August 1938 at Malta, transferred his flag back to the *Barham* on 9 January 1939. The *Hood* had a complement of 1341 officers and men, but with the staff embarked the numbers were even greater. One of the Malta traditions was to have a photograph of the ship's company, and here the majority of the *Hood's* complement together with the Admiral and his staff cover the forward end of the superstructure. The ship's trophies are given place of honour between the barrels of A turret and her massive cables for her anchors are in the foreground. It is sad to reflect that all but three of her crew were lost when she was sunk by the *Bismarck* on 24 May 1941, and this photograph shows the magnitude of that disaster in human terms.

Overleaf

FLEET IN HARBOUR
15 April 1939

The *Queen Elizabeth* Class Battleship *Warspite* (see page 137) is in the foreground of this view, wearing the Commander-in-Chief's flag and showing clearly her recent modifications. Beyond her can be seen her sister ship, the *Barham*. The *Barham* did not receive the major rebuilding that others of her class were given, though she was fitted with two twin 4 inch anti-aircraft guns on each side. She has a tripod mainmast and also has a catapult fitted on X turret. She was torpedoed by U331 off Sollum on 25 November 1941 with the loss of 862 officers and men. The Destroyer Depot Ship *Woolwich* lies astern of the *Warspite*. Launched by Fairfield in September 1934, her 4 inch guns were sited amidships abreast her funnels. She survived the war and was broken up in 1962 at Dalmuir. Astern of her is the *County* Class Cruiser *Shropshire*, flagship of the First Cruiser Squadron. One of the *London* Group, she was transferred to Australia in 1943 to replace the *Canberra*. Astern of her is a sister ship, the *Devonshire*. The third member of the First Cruiser Squadron was the *Sussex*, who left Malta on 23 May to collect a draft of 300 men for Alexandria, having had her self refit curtailled. Moored by the floating dock is a *Gloucester* Class Cruiser, probably the *Liverpool*, which had been commissioned on 2 November 1938, had arrived at Malta on 20 January 1939 and was undergoing rectification to main engine defects. Her sister ship, the *Gloucester*, had arrived at Malta on 23 March and was also having adjustments made to her flexible couplings. She had been completed at Devonport on 31 January. Both ships reached Aden on 2 May.

BIGHI BAY
1939

This panorama of Bighi Bay taken in 1939 shows a mixture of types and ages of ships. In the foreground is the battleship *Ramillies* (see page 122), with her high torpedo bulges and twin 4 inch anti-aircraft guns added between the wars. She was still in the Mediterranean on the outbreak of war. Beyond her can be seen the battleship *Malaya*, (see page 130), also modernised between the wars though not as extensively as some of her sister ships. She was also in the Mediterranean at the start of the war. She was more involved in the war in the Mediterranean, being part of Force H for a time. Both took part in the bombardment of Normandy before becoming tenders to *HMS Vernon* at Portsmouth. The aircraft carrier on the left is the *Glorious*, launched in 1916 as a heavy cruiser and converted to an aircraft carrier between 1924 and 1930. She was sunk by the *Scharnhorst* and *Gneisenau* off Norway in June 1940 with heavy loss of life. Beyond her can be seen the three funnels of a *County* Class cruiser, either the *Sussex* or the *Shropshire*, whilst lying in Kalkara Creek is the Tribal Class destroyer *Cossack*, which had completed to full complement on 14 June 1938 for the First Tribal Destroyer Flotilla. She gained fame under the command of Captain P L Vian off Norway and in the action against the *Bismarck* before being torpedoed with the loss of her Captain and 158 men West of Gibraltar in October 1941.

HMS ZULU
30 July 1939

Completed on 6 September 1938 and commissioned with a Devonport crew, the *Zulu* is seen here leaving Grand Harbour for Istanbul and Limissol after a period of docking. Her fine lines and heavy gun armament of four twin 4.7 inch guns look splendid, but the low angle of elevation of her main armament was to be a penalty in the war, and later a twin 4 inch AA gun was mounted in X position instead of the twin 4.7 inch. The quadruple pom pom mounted forward of the seachlight by the mainmast and the machine guns between the funnels were insufficient anti-aircraft defence. She did not return to Malta after visiting Limassol, but sailed for Portland, returning to Malta on 28 September 1941. She was one of Captain Vian's 4th Flotilla that engaged the *Bismarck* in the early hours of 27 May 1941. In March 42 she took part in the Second Battle of Sirte, when Vian, then a Rear Admiral, carried out a determined and successful defence of a Malta bound convoy against superior Italian forces. In August 1942 she helped sink U372 off Jaffa. The next month she was involved in a raid on Tobruk. Her sister ship the *Sikh* was hit by shore batteries and *Zulu* was unable to tow her clear, so *Sikh* was lost. The cruiser *Coventry* (see page 94) was bombed whilst supporting *Zulu's* withdrawal and the *Zulu* was hit in the engine room by the last bomb dropped in the last attack, and sank that night.

THE MEDITERRANEAN

THE MAIN HARBOURS, MALTA

Tigne
Manoel Island
MARSAMXETT HARBOUR
Valletta
GRAND HARBOUR
Marsa

Note: The names of places are spelt as in the text, although there were variations in use, and many have since had their names altered.

KEY TO THE MEDITERRANEAN

Adriatic	1	Corfu	18	Mentone	35	Sea of Mamara	52
Aegean	2	Crete	19	Monopoli	36	Sevastapol	53
Alexandretta	3	Dardanelles	20	Mudros	37	Smyrna	54
Alexandria	4	Doro Channel	21	Naples	38	Spalato	55
Algiers	5	Dragamesti Bay	22	Novorossisk	39	Suda Bay	56
Argostoli	6	Durazzo	23	Odessa	40	Tangiers	57
Astakos	7	Elba	24	Oran	41	Taranto	58
Balearic Islands	8	Galatz	25	Palermo	42	Trebrond	59
Barcelona	9	Gibralter	26	Palma	43	Valencia	60
Beirut	10	Gulf of Xeros	27	Patras	44	Valona	61
Biograd	11	Ierissos	28	Phaleron	45	Venice	62
Black Sea	12	Istanbul	17	Platea	46	Villefranche	63
Bona	13	Kephalo	30	Pollensa	47	Zante	64
Brindisi	14	Kotor	31	Port Said	48	Zaverda	65
Catania	15	Limassol	32	Premuda Is	49		
Chanak	16	Malta	33	Salamis Bay	50		
Constantinople	17	Marseilles	34	Salonica	51		

KEY TO THE MAIN HARBOURS, MALTA

Barracca Garden	1	Fort St Angelo	7	Ricasoli Point	13
Bighi	2	French Creek	8	Rinella Creek	14
Corradino Heights	3	Kalkara Creek	9	St Elmo Point	15
Customs House Landing	4	Lazaretto Creek	10	St Julian's Point	16
Dockyard Creek	5	Msida Creek	11	Senglea	17
Dragutt Point	6	Pieta Creek	12		

INDEX

Named ships, with launch dates in brackets, showing page number